DATE DUE	
~~MAR 12 2008~~		
~~MAY 03 2010~~		

D1511313

IN THE
SHOGUN'S
SHADOW

OTHER BOOKS BY JOHN LANGONE

AIDS
The Facts

Bombed, Buzzed, Smashed, or . . . Sober
A Book about Alcohol

Dead End
A Book about Suicide

Death Is a Noun
A View of the End of Life

Goodbye to Bedlam
Understanding Mental Illness and Retardation

Growing Older
What Young People Should Know about Aging

Human Engineering
Marvel or Menace?

Life at the Bottom
The People of Antarctica

Like, Love, Lust
A View of Sex and Sexuality

Long Life
What We Know and Are Learning about the Aging Process

Our Endangered Earth
What We Can Do to Save It

Spreading Poison
A Book about Racism and Prejudice

Thorny Issues
How Ethics and Morality Affect the Way We Live

Violence!
Our Fastest-Growing Health Problem

Vital Signs
The Way We Die in America

IN THE SHOGUN'S SHADOW

Understanding a Changing Japan

John Langone

Illustrated by Steven Parton

Little, Brown and Company
Boston   New York   Toronto   London

For my uncle, George Consolazio

Text copyright © 1994 by John Langone
Illustrations copyright © 1994 by Steven Parton

First Edition

Excerpts from "Teen Tokyo: Youth and Popular Culture" by permission
of the Children's Museum, Boston, and Ozone, Inc.

Library of Congress Cataloging-in-Publication Data

Langone, John, 1929–
    In the shogun's shadow : understanding a changing Japan / John
Langone ; illustrated by Steven Parton. — First ed.
        p.   cm.
    Includes index.
    ISBN 0-316-51409-8
    1. Japan — Civilization — 1945– — Juvenile literature.   2. Japan —
Relations — United States — Juvenile literature.   3. United States —
Relations — Japan — Juvenile literature.   I. Title.
DS822.5.L36   1994
952 — dc20   93-23999

10 9 8 7 6 5 4 3 2 1

RRD-VA

Published simultaneously in Canada
by Little, Brown & Company (Canada) Limited

Printed in the United States of America

Contents

Preface: What Do You Know about the Japanese?   vii

Introduction: Zipangu, Jih-pen, Dai Nippon   xiii

Part One: Japan's Geography and History

   1. Mountains and People   3

   2. Gods and Goddesses; Emperors and Shoguns   16

   3. Foreign Devils, Black Ships, and an
      American Shogun   30

Part Two: Modern Japanese Society

   4. Beliefs and Customs   43

   5. Japanese Home Life   50

   6. Sex and Sex Roles in Japan   58

   7. The Youth of Japan   74

   8. The Industrious Japanese   99

   9. Even Workaholics Take Time Out   114

  10. Crime, *Koban,* and the *Yakuza*   124

Part Three: U.S.–Japanese Relations

  11. What Americans Think of the Japanese   139

  12. What the Japanese Think of Us and
      Other *Gaijin*   148

  13. What the Japanese Think of Themselves   159

14. What the Japanese Don't Say about Themselves 165

15. Getting Along with the Japanese 173

Appendix: Spoken and Unspoken Language 179

Notes 189

Index 195

What Do You Know about the Japanese?

Before you start turning the pages, let's see what you know and don't know about Japan and the people who live there. The answers to the following one hundred true-or-false questions, or at least clues to the answers, will be found in this book, and some of them may surprise you. When you go through the list, try to answer *yes* or *no,* but don't be afraid to respond with an occasional *sometimes* or *don't know.*

1. Japan is larger than the United States.
2. The Japanese work longer hours than we do.
3. The Japanese are smarter than we are.
4. The Japanese are like no one else on earth.
5. All Japanese women prefer to wear kimonos.
6. There's no crime in Japan.
7. Japanese wives are interested only in housework.
8. Japanese teenagers don't ever rebel.
9. The Japanese language comes from Chinese.

10. Japanese students spend more time in school than American students do.
11. There are no homeless people in Japan.
12. Japanese workers generally stay with one company all their life.
13. Buddhism is Japan's only religion.
14. There is capital punishment in Japan.
15. Japan grows most of its own food.
16. Japan is mostly mountains.
17. There is no racial or ethnic prejudice in Japan.
18. The Japanese don't import a lot of American products.
19. Americans fear and distrust the Japanese.
20. The Japanese are buying up all of America.
21. American companies don't do well in Japan.
22. Abortion is not common in Japan.
23. The average Japanese family has five kids.
24. Japanese homes are smaller than ours.
25. Japan got its constitution from the United States.
26. The Japanese used to believe their emperor was a god.
27. The emperor rules the country.
28. Consumer goods are very expensive in Japan.
29. Japan has no minorities.
30. Most Japanese have black hair.
31. Japan has always welcomed foreigners.
32. Japan is one large island in the Pacific Ocean.
33. Japan is a part of the Asian mainland.
34. Japanese women usually marry by the time they're twenty-five.
35. The Japanese invented the VCR.

36. The Japanese invented automobiles.
37. The Japanese are very independent and individualistic.
38. Japanese teens have higher IQs than American teens.
39. The Japanese don't relax much.
40. Japan was believed to have been created by gods and goddesses.
41. Japanese kids don't care much for American fashions and fads.
42. Japanese kids respect American kids' individuality.
43. Japan's government is more like ours than like China's.
44. There are no women in Japanese politics.
45. Most Japanese don't regard Americans as their friends.
46. The Japanese are unfair traders.
47. Japan is a stronger economic power than the United States.
48. Japanese workers are far more productive than American workers.
49. All Japanese are short.
50. The Japanese have great respect for family values.
51. The Japanese are mostly imitators.
52. Japanese teenagers never hassle their fellow students.
53. There is drug abuse in Japan.
54. Japanese use only chopsticks when they eat.
55. You can get a Big Mac in Japan.
56. The Japanese drive on the left side of the road, as in England.
57. A Japanese book is read from the right to the left.
58. Most Japanese students wear uniforms.

59. In Japan, college students study harder than high school students.
60. Japanese students aren't very good at memorizing facts.
61. Very few foreigners live in Japan.
62. The police are not very well liked in Japan.
63. Japanese mothers push their kids hard to study.
64. Japanese fathers don't usually help with the housework.
65. The Japanese respect the elderly.
66. Japanese students never disagree with their teachers.
67. Japan has indigenous people like our Native Americans.
68. The Japanese eat a lot of fish.
69. Japanese teenagers don't believe in having sex before marriage.
70. Japanese teachers are less strict than ours.
71. There is no pornography or prostitution in Japan.
72. Japan has strict gun control laws.
73. Most marriages in Japan are arranged by families.
74. Japanese teens don't hang out.
75. In Japan, men have more rights than women.
76. There is no divorce in Japan.
77. There is no birth control in Japan.
78. Japan's population is larger than ours.
79. Most of Japan's people live in cities.
80. Japan's farmers are a powerful group.
81. Japan's climate is like ours.
82. Japan has the same kinds of flowers and trees that we do.
83. Very few Japanese live overseas.

84. A bow to a Japanese means the same as shaking hands to us.
85. The Japanese don't have any military forces.
86. The Japanese have a lot of minerals and oil.
87. Japan's unemployment rate is as high as ours.
88. In Japan, workers' pay is based more on length of service than on ability.
89. Japan doesn't have many railroads.
90. The Japanese save more money than we do.
91. Alcohol is forbidden in Japan.
92. Real estate is cheaper in Japan than in the U.S.
93. There are no nuclear power plants in Japan.
94. The Japanese constitution gives equal rights to women.
95. Japan was trying to build an atomic bomb during World War II.
96. The Japanese smile when they are uncomfortable or embarrassed.
97. Shame is not very important to the Japanese.
98. Japanese students are taught about Japan's role in World War II.
99. The Japanese say exactly what they think.
100. The Japanese don't like hugging, kissing, or loud laughter in public.

Introduction

Zipangu, Jih-pen, Dai Nippon

Japan, a collection of islands in the Pacific Ocean off the east coast of Asia, has had many names. When Marco Polo, the Venetian traveler and adventurer, visited the island kingdom in 1295, he called it Zipangu, which was his mispronunciation of the Chinese name for the islands, Jih-pen, meaning "source of the sun." The residents of the islands called their homeland Dai Nippon, which meant Great Land of the Rising Sun.

To the Chinese, living across the sea from Japan, and to the Japanese themselves, the sun did, indeed, appear to rise over the islands each day. To ancient peoples, this was more than just an astronomical event. Preindustrial peoples were acutely aware of the sun as the source of light and heat and life. They worshiped the sun as a god, and the rising sun represented the ascendancy of greatness. A setting sun, on the other hand, meant decline. As the Roman statesman Pompey saw it, "More worship the rising than the setting sun." And Shakespeare wrote, "Men shut their doors against a setting sun."

Modern-day Japan has fulfilled the glowing promise of the sun that rises over it with each dawn. Today, Japan is the economic and industrial powerhouse of Asia, a titan whose strength and influence are felt around the globe to an extent that is way out of proportion to the country's relatively small size and population and to its scant natural resources. This island nation is a world leader in the manufacture of automobiles, electronics, and ships, and some of the fastest trains on earth. But Japan is far more than a massive factory churning out consumer goods and the means to transport them, more than "Japan, Inc.," the nickname that American industrialists — sometimes enviously, sometimes bitterly — have pinned on it. And, contrary to popular opinion in the West, Japan is a lot more than a mere copying machine that prints out facsimiles of other people's work and has never had a bright and original idea of its own.

Japan has contributed much more than Toyota and Honda cars, NEC computers, Toshiba laptops, JVC VCRs, Canon cameras and copiers, Hitachi TVs, Shiseido perfume, Sony Walkmen, and Panasonic stereos. It gave us the world's first, and one of its greatest, novels, *The Tale of Genji,* written between 1000 and 1020 A.D. by a noblewoman; it gave us Kabuki and No drama; the tea ceremony; landscape gardening; the style of flower arrangement known as ikebana; miniature bonsai trees; Zen Buddhism; charcoal cooking with hibachis; sushi; tatami mats; shoji screens; the paintings of Hokusai; "Rashomon" and other famous stories by Akutagawa; and, currently, the films of director Akira Kurosawa and the concert music of Seiji Ozawa, conductor of the Boston Symphony Orchestra. In science and medicine, as well as industry, Japan's researchers are among the world's best and brightest. The efficient management style of its companies has been copied by many of our own. Even its baseball teams get high marks: many have beaten America's best in exhibition games.

Japan today is a far cry from the Japan that, before World War II, was known mainly for the cheap toys and knickknacks whose stamp, "Made in Japan," was just another name for junk. It is more than the picturesque inns, rustic bridges, and carved-wood balconies hung with paper lanterns that appear on posters in airlines offices. Japan is a modern nation of notable contributions and traits, none the least of which are patience and determination. For not only did the country literally rise up out of the ashes of World War II to survive, but it showed the world — albeit with the help of the United States, which had conquered it — that it could rise to a position of dominance in less than fifty years. "Americans tend to give themselves credit for the postwar transformation of Japan," Edwin O. Reischauer, former U.S. ambassador to Japan, has written,

and certainly American occupation policy did help to set the course, but other factors were even more important in determining what happened. Without the Japanese people's capacity for hard work and cooperation, their universal literacy, their high levels of government efficiency, their great organizational skills and industrial knowhow, and their considerable experience with the democratic institutions of elections and parliamentary government, the American reforms would probably have sunk into a sea of confusion. If the Japanese had not turned their backs emphatically on militarism and authoritarian rule themselves, American efforts at reform might well have ended in complete frustration.[1]

The Japanese are a truly remarkable people, a population that clings to old ways as readily as it embraces new ones. They are, unlike Americans, a homogeneous group — that is, they are and have been for the most part a people whose language, traditions, race, and religion are shared by virtually all Japanese and are not mixed with non-Japanese. This centuries-old homogeneity, part of it due to Japan's past geographic isolation from the rest of the world, has worked to the country's advantage because it has freed the nation from the sort of racial and ethnic friction and disputes that tear many other countries apart. Look at what's been happening in Eastern Europe with the demise of communism and the Soviet Union, and in countries outside what was known as the Soviet bloc. Factional disputes — ethnic, political, and religious — rage in the Balkans, Afghanistan, Lebanon, and India. Even in the United States, "land of the free," race riots touched off by hatred between African-Americans and whites erupt every so often, and various ethnic groups are regularly attacked or harassed by bigots. The sameness of the Japanese has shielded them from such events, and it also allows them to work easily as a group — a goal in direct contrast to the tenets of Western philosophies, which often emphasize the individual to the detriment of the greater good.

There is, however, also a down side to the way Japan conducts itself. The nation's clannishness often makes the Japanese fearful and mistrustful of foreigners and insensitive to their needs and beliefs; it has made many Japanese feel superior to others, and sometimes intolerant even of Japanese who are not driven by the noble spirit — the inborn quality of dignity that the Japanese call *hinkaku* — or who may be physically or mentally disabled and are, therefore, less than "perfect" or, as some Japanese put it, "damaged goods." The nation's drive to be number one has resulted, at this writing, in bad investments and risk taking that have slowed down the economy, forced a record number of corporations into bankruptcy, and caused banks to suffer losses from bad loans to businessmen who were interested only in accumulating more wealth and property.

This is a book about Japan, and the Japanese people. But although it contains essential facts and figures, it aims to be more than a geography book or a travel guide. It is also a book of impressions of Japan, an attempt to peer beneath what is to most Westerners a strange and incomprehensible culture. For many years, our junior high and high school history books focused only on Rome, Egypt, and medieval Europe. The other side of the globe, where Japan and China are situated, was generally ignored. Their cultures were, yes, remote, but they were ancient, distinct, and in some ways far superior to those more familiar to us. One travel writer who visited Japan in the late 1800s had this to say about the East:

> *When the traveler visits China, India, and Japan, he begins to feel as men might who, having always thought the Rhine to be the only river of any magnitude on earth, should suddenly find themselves beside the Nile, whose mighty volume has been rolling onward for unnumbered ages, and over whose distant origin there hangs the halo of mystery.*[2]

Because there are so many myths and misconceptions in the West about Japan and its people, and because many of you will be dealing more with the Japanese than your parents have, it is important these days for young people especially to know more about Japan than what appears in standard reference works. In the pages ahead, we'll discuss the cultural differences between

Japanese and Americans, but we'll also note the similarities that many Westerners are either ignorant of or pay little attention to because they believe that the Japanese are truly "different" and "inscrutable." We'll compare the education of Japanese students to the way you are taught, and learn whether Japanese kids really are "smarter." We'll look at crime and violence in Japan, which most Americans believe is always peaceful and crime-free; at what young Japanese people want to do with their lives; at how some are becoming more Westernized and at what that is doing to Japanese society; and at what Japanese teens think of Americans. In short, the book is a sort of behavioral digest that tries to be as honest as it can as it focuses not only on Japan's glories, the confidence of its people, and the nation's reverence for harmony, but on the problems the country faces, on the fierce pressures Japanese society places on its youth and its workers — on a nation torn, as no other is, between the old and the new, between the potter's wheel and the blast furnace, between the abacus and the computer, between kimono-clad geishas and leather-jacketed motorcycle gangs, the moat-encircled emperor's palace in the center of Tokyo and the golden arches of McDonald's.

Japan is a land of rich culture, and a look at some of the customary beliefs, rituals, and behavior that are part of that culture will help you better understand why Japanese act and think as they do. Life is not always bright in the Land of the Rising Sun, and an honest look at some of Japan's difficulties and at some aspects of society that many Japanese would rather keep hidden will not only give you a more realistic view of our closest Asian friends but will also demonstrate that in many ways, the Japanese are not really all that different from us. As humans, after all, we share many things, no matter our racial and ethnic backgrounds.

Yes, to many Westerners the Japanese seem to do things upside down and inside out. They serve their fish raw, and we eat it cooked; Japanese women hold umbrellas and doors for men, whereas we have traditionally expected men to do so for women; Japanese wear white at funerals, and we wear black; they take your shoes at the door of their homes instead of your hat and coat; they read books from our back to our front; they heat their wine, and we serve ours chilled; they pull saws only toward them, and we go back and forth; our keys turn outward, theirs inward; they mount horses from the right, and we do it from the left; many of them still sleep on the floor and eat at low tables while kneeling on the floor; they plant trees in flowerpots; they bow instead of shaking hands.

But as strange as the Japanese may seem to some of us — and don't forget that Americans are as strange and incomprehensible to the Japanese as they are to us — they have the same basic feelings and needs that we do; they have similar goals and enjoy the same kind of social relations we do. Like anyone, they can be kind and thoughtful or unkind and thoughtless. They love and laugh, grieve and hate, just as we do. Sometimes they do not express their emotions in the same way we do, but they do feel them. What's important to remember, too, is that the Japanese are not all the same. And they are constantly changing, just as we change. Many of Japan's young people are rebelling against the old ways; many want more out of life, for better or worse, than what their often restrictive society allows them.

It is hoped that this book will help you to learn something from the Japanese. They have most certainly been influenced by

America's spirit of creativity and by our inventions — everything from baseball to computers to the VCR — and Americans should be equally willing to learn from all the things that are distinctively Japanese: their attitudes toward work and education and society; their reluctance to seek simple, quick solutions; their willingness to wait for what is worth waiting for; the care they take with even little things; their courtesy and refinement. Ideally, once we understand each other better and open up the lines of communication, the best aspects of our cultures can be shared and adopted for the benefit of both countries.

Part One

Japan's Geography and History

1

Mountains and People

On a map, continents and other land masses sometimes resemble familiar objects, animals, or even people. Cape Cod, Massachusetts, looks something like a flexed arm; Italy like a boot; Scotland, England, and Wales like an old woman in a long dress and a bonnet; South America like an ice cream cone.

If you let your imagination continue to run wild, Japan can be seen as a fire-breathing dragon. The flames spouting from the dragon's mouth are Russia's Kuril Islands. The dragon's head is snow-swept Hokkaido, one of the four main islands of Japan and its least populated. The dragon's midsection is the island of Honshu, home to some 80 percent of the Japanese people and the site of the country's capital, Tokyo. The island of Shikoku, an agricultural region, might be considered the dragon's lower legs, and Kyushu, a subtropical island, the tail. There are nearly four thousand smaller islands, including Okinawa, which was occupied by the United States after World War II and returned to Japan in 1972.

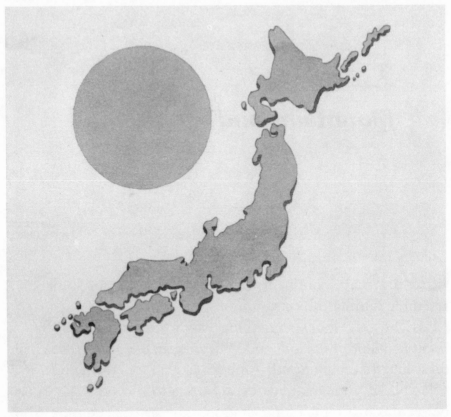

Map of Japan

In overall size, Japan's four largest islands cover as much area as New England, New York, and Pennsylvania combined; or, for another perspective, Japan is as large as Montana and a bit smaller than California. If you look at a map, you'll see that Japan is in the same latitude as the east coast of the United States, stretching from northern New England to Georgia. The climate is much like that of our east coast, with four distinctive seasons, varying weather conditions in the north and south, and plenty of rainfall. Tourists usually pick the spring to visit Japan because it is the season of flowers — plum and peach trees blossom in early March, followed by the big floral event that is eagerly awaited every year, the blooming of the cherry trees. Many flowers and trees in Japan are quite familiar to Americans — cedars, beeches, magnolias, pines, oaks, chrysanthemums, violets, azaleas, and morning glories, to name a few. The animal life, too, is not all that unusual — except for a few unique native animals like the *habu,* a poisonous snake, and the *yamaneko,* a breed of wildcat; there are also monkeys, boars, black bears, ducks, pheasants, and foxes.

If that general picture were all that we had, Japan wouldn't seem much different from where many of us live in the United States. But Japan lacks something that we in America take for granted: usable land. While Japan is certainly not the smallest of countries, the amount of land it has for agriculture is minuscule: around 20 percent. The rest is forested mountains that run straight down the middle of the four islands and sometimes spread outward right down to the Pacific Ocean on one side and the Sea of Japan on the other. The highest mountain is world-famous Fuji-san, an inactive volcano 12,385 feet high. There are other volcanoes — in fact, Japan has a tenth of the active ones in the world — and these erupt frequently and cause a great deal of damage. Earthquakes, too, occur fairly often, and over the centuries, massive temblors have wracked the nation: among the most notable were the quake of 1891, which killed 10,000 people and left 300,000 homeless, and one in 1923, which destroyed all of Yokohama and 70 percent of Tokyo, killing more than 150,000 people and wrecking a million homes.

What little fertile land Japan does have is harvested with incredible efficiency in what resemble backyard gardens and on

Hillside farms

terraced hillsides that use every inch of arable soil. But it is nowhere near enough, and the country must import much of its food. Even fish, which used to be plentiful in the waters around the country and is the major source of protein for the Japanese — who eat more fish than anyone on earth — is scarce nowadays. The seas around Japan are rapidly becoming fished out, and large Japanese fleets roam the world looking for catches.

If the food problem were not enough of a setback, Japan also has very little, and in many cases none at all, of the minerals essential to industry. Iron ore, aluminum, tin, copper, lead, and zinc must all be bought from other countries in order to keep Japan's factories humming. Energy is also a problem. Japan has only a little natural gas and coal, and no oil, and so it must import some 90 percent of the fuels it needs. Compare that rather dismal picture with the United States, which has vast tracts of farmland, huge mineral deposits, enough coal to take us well into the twenty-fourth century, and 3 percent of the world's estimated trillion barrels of oil (we import 50 percent of our oil).

The lack of agricultural land and the dominance of mountains also mean that there is very little space for people to live, work, and play in. Floor space per person in the U.S. is perhaps twice what it is in Japan. When someone builds a house in a Tokyo suburb, he or she will have to pay twice as much for the land as for building the house.

Japan's population is around 124 million, the seventh largest in the world behind China, India, the former Soviet Union, the United States (with a current population of around 250 million), Indonesia, and Brazil. This means that Japan has more people than each of the Big Four countries of Western Europe: Great Britain, Germany, France, and Italy. All those people packed for the most part into major cities makes Japan one of the most densely populated countries on earth.

Of Japan's cities Tokyo has the largest population, nearly 12 million, followed by Osaka, another major business center, with nearly nine million. The falling birth rate in Japan has slowed population growth somewhat, but that is offset by the fact that the Japanese are living longer: Japan now has the world's highest average life expectancy, 82.5 years for women, and 76.2 years for men.

Fitting so many people into a few large cities requires some doing, and the Japanese have snuggled efficiently — if not always comfortably — into the limited amount of space. Skyscrapers abound, of course, and the skylines in major cities are not all that different from those in U.S. metropolises, except that many of the glowing multicolored neon signs imprint the heavens with distinctive Japanese characters, which are incomprehensible to most Western eyes. Looking out over Tokyo from the top of an office building or hotel makes you realize that the city is one of the world's greatest, a bustling center of business, finance, politics, education, culture, and fashion. The well-dressed crowds, the maze of streets, the lovely shops and elegant department stores full of luxury items of every description and from every country on earth, many English signs among the Japanese ones, loudspeakers sending out rock, jazz, and classical music, the pounding of pile drivers, and the dazzling nightlife, all make it very hard to believe that the city was enemy territory during World War II and was leveled during that war.

A Westerner does notice things that are, however, peculiarly Japanese. First, the people are generally smaller than most Americans, and just about everything they use seems to be scaled down. Second, space is limited. If anyone on earth knows how to get the most out of cramped quarters, it is the Japanese. Go into any of their apartments, restaurants, stores, or gardens and you'll be very embarrassed at how much space we Americans waste. One of our high-ceilinged homes or stores would make two levels in Japan; one of our closets would make a work space, even a bedroom. Few Japanese families can hold large dinner parties or even have a few people over because their rooms aren't big enough for many more than the family. Not only are Japanese apartments tiny by our standards, but the furniture and appliances are sized accordingly as well. A typical washing machine is so light and small it can be moved easily with one hand from one room to another. Many Japanese sleep on quilted mattresses called futons. Laid on soft floors made of grass matting, called tatami, the mattresses can be rolled up after use, something you cannot do with a standard bed, which both takes up a lot of space and wastes it, since beds are not generally in use throughout the day. Chairs in restaurants and coffee shops are undersized to accommodate people generally shorter than Americans, and jammed into space that makes sitting down and getting up extremely difficult for someone not used

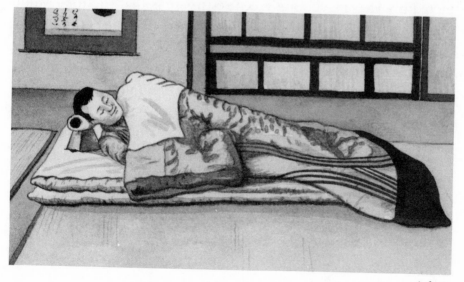

A futon

to it. So crowded are many restaurants that patrons have to wait in line out on the street until their table is ready. Aisles in many shops are so narrow that a visitor almost needs a shoehorn to move around in them; drinking fountains in parks are so low that for many Americans, a deep knee bend is necessary to reach the water spout; pizzas are the size of apple pies; coffee isn't served in mugs but in delicate cups; newspapers have only between four and a dozen pages; minitrucks, minivans, and "easy-to-ride motorcycles for little riders" roll through the narrow streets. Even Japanese tobacco pipes are lilliputian: with bowls about the size of a thimble, they hold enough tobacco for just three puffs.

The smallness of many things in Japan is, of course, born out of necessity — huge pizzas, naturally, require huge ovens and even bigger buildings to contain the ovens. And constructing a large building in Japan is virtually impossible unless you have an enormous amount of money, because available land is incredibly expensive: one recent estimate is that the total value of all the land is around $15 trillion, some five times that of the whole United States.[1] At the going price of around $200,000 for a mere square yard of prime commercial space in Tokyo, it's doubtful a pizza business could afford a big, fancy building and the ovens to turn out pizzas like the ones we're used to here. The small scale of things in Japan is evidence of the nation's uncanny ability to adapt to difficult circumstances, and to come up with solutions and the craftsmanship to put them in effect.

The smallness is also indicative of something else: the people's appreciation of delicate things, and their skill in making what is small seem big. We'll discuss Japanese tastes a bit later, but we can say here that bulky items not only don't fit well in Japanese apartments and homes, they are not regarded as especially attractive. Japanese food is simple and light, not elaborate and heavy, but when a classic dish is carefully arranged on a gorgeously painted platter, the meal looks like a banquet; Japanese sentences can be quite short, sometimes without subjects, but full of meaning; a rock in a Japanese garden is enough to give the impression of a mountain; a small pool of water becomes a lake; the three spare lines in a traditional haiku poem speak volumes; silk embroidery and gold brocade, all done with fine needles, splash as much color as an artist's broad brush heavily loaded with thick oil paint.

Here's how one traveler to Japan in the late 1800s described the meticulous preparation of a work of cloisonné, a style of enamel decoration:

> *Taking a copper vase, the artist traces on its surface certain figures, such as flowers, birds, and trees. Then, from a roll of brass, one-sixteenth of an inch in breadth, he cuts off tiny pieces which, with consummate skill, and by eye-measurement alone, he twists into a mass of lines which correspond exactly to the figures he has drawn. Holding these bits of brass between the points of tweezers, he touches them with glue, and deftly locates them upon the rounded surface of the vase. At length, when all the figures are outlined, as it were, in skeleton, the flesh has to be applied. The thousands of spaces between the lines of brass are filled with enamel of all shades and colors. When this is done, the jar is placed into a furnace, then touched with more enamel, then fired again, and so on, till it has been brought to the required degree of artistic finish. Then it is polished with great care, until the shining edges of the brass show through the*

enamel like the veins of a leaf. The colors also, by this time, are perfectly distinct and permanent, and the entire work stands forth, a marvelous combination of delicacy, strength and beauty.[2]

It is no wonder that one of Japan's most popular proverbs is *Do yori kimo ga haru* — "The best things come in small packages."

The proverb might apply to Japan itself. With its buildings crowded close to one another and its people hemmed in and squeezed out by mountains, the country is, when measured against other superpowers, a small package indeed. But it is enviably resourceful. Japan's gardens, as we have said, produce a good supply of fruits and vegetables — with only about 8 percent of its working population farming them. While Japan is forced to import rice, one of its dietary staples, its own rice yield is among the world's largest, even with tiny farms. Japan is also developing ways to increase fish supplies by raising fish and shellfish on marine farms; and it is working hard to improve its energy situation by improving nuclear power (thirty-nine nuclear reactors already generate around 30 percent of the nation's electricity) and developing new forms of energy such as coal liquefaction, and geothermal and solar energy.

Transporting the Japanese is as difficult as feeding and housing them. But here again, the Japanese have made an art out of a necessity. The country has an extensive network of railways, which is the chief form of national transportation, and there are subways and bus systems as well. Daily commuting is an ordeal in Japan's large cities — the three busiest rail terminals in Japan, including Tokyo's, move nearly a million and a half people every day — but the many trains run every few minutes during rush hours, are clean, and have a remarkable safety record, with hardly an accident for the billions of passenger miles they travel every year. They are also precisely on time. A foreign visitor who, after checking a wristwatch, informs a station attendant that a train is late, is apt to be told, "Train not late, watch late." *logic* The Japanese are proud of the sophisticated technology and maintenance that keep their trains running so efficiently. If a motorman ignores a red stop signal, alarms go off, and if they are ignored, an automatic brake halts the train; train and subway stations have electronic ticket sellers and ticket takers; to help passengers keep directions straight in their minds, male announcers give information for one direction, females for the opposite one — all over a stereo system. The Japanese transportation experts have also made sure that a visitor won't get lost while riding the train around Tokyo: the Yamanote line makes a circle around the center of the city, clockwise and counterclockwise, stopping at all the key stations; if you miss a stop, just stay aboard, and you'll return in about an hour.

The pride of the Japanese railway system is the Shinkansen, the so-called bullet train. These high-speed super-express trains are capable of traveling almost silently and without vibration at more than one hundred miles an hour, and they run the length of the country. The safety measures they employ are good examples of the impressive technology the Japanese rely on: wind and earthquake detectors and rain gauges are installed along the entire line to warn of impending natural disasters; in case of an earthquake, the current is automatically shut down, and the trains in the danger area stop; if there is high wind or heavy rain, the train's running speed is automatically reduced, or the train is stopped; the trains' windows are made of double-layered glass with air space between to lessen noise, wind pressure, and condensation. In the future, Japan will undoubtedly be running even faster trains, trains without wheels that literally

A bullet train

fly over magnetic rails like magic carpets. Experimental versions of such trains, called maglevs, short for magnetic levitation, are already in use in Japan.

It might seem surprising that the Japanese rely so heavily on public transportation; all of the Japanese cars on our streets give the impression that the Japanese use them as much as we do. The Japanese do drive, of course, and the number of motor vehicles in Japan has increased: from about 1.5 million in 1960 to some 60 million today. (The U.S. has about 140 million passenger cars.) But because of the lack of space, traffic jams are mammoth and driving a car can be a constant source of stress. To help the pedestrians, who have to cross streets in the midst of snarled and zigzagging traffic, the city of Tokyo has installed more than 1,000 overhead pedestrian crosswalks, far more than exist in any other city in Europe or America. They apparently work, because pedestrian deaths in Tokyo are the lowest of any city.

Despite the traffic jams, the overcrowding, and the scarcity of fertile farmland, however, Japan is far from being a country in need of repair. Just as the Japanese people make do with what little farmland they do have, and manage nicely to feed, house, and transport themselves, so, too, have they been able to supply much of the world with top-quality industrial and consumer goods. Japan manufactures and exports some of the best cars, electronics, and appliances the world has ever known. The care the Japanese take when manufacturing all of these goods is almost as painstaking as the work that went into the ancient art of cloisonné.

In the pages ahead we'll look at some of the elements that make up the culture that shapes Japan, its people, and the work they do — history, religion, philosophy, art, politics, education, science, fads, trends, values, and attitudes. We'll try to see what makes the Japanese tick. And, it is hoped, you will see that there is far more to the Japanese than what Marco Polo wrote about them during his very brief stay in their country:

> *The people are fair-complexioned, good-looking, and well-mannered. They are idolaters, wholly independent and exercising no authority over any nation but themselves. They have gold in great abundance, because it is found there in measureless quantities. And I assure you that no one exports it from the island, because no trader, nor indeed anyone else, goes there from the mainland.*[3]

2

Gods and Goddesses; Emperors and Shoguns

When Marco Polo observed that nobody went to Japan from the mainland, he was correct — for his day. For centuries at a time, Japan was an isolated nation, a mysterious group of islands whose people, customs, and history were as obscure as a fog-shrouded harbor.

Fog-shrouded is still an appropriate characterization for Japan's early history, which is much different from our own. In 1976, for example, we marked the bicentennial of the United States, the two hundredth anniversary of our country's birth. We know that Thomas Jefferson drafted the Declaration of Independence, and we have documented historical records of everyone else who participated in the formation of our nation. George Washington, John Adams, John Hancock, Benjamin Franklin, and all the other colonial statesmen are household names to Americans.

But now consider Japan. It has two histories, a legendary one and a historical one. On the calendar of world events, both histories make our founding seem as though it occurred only last

16

week and the study of American history seem like a piece of cake. Japan's history supposedly began many hundreds of years before Christ with a god named Izanagi and his sister, the goddess Izanami. Floating to earth from their home in heaven, they dipped a jeweled spear into the ocean, raised it, and shook it in the sky. The drops of salt water that sprayed from the spear became, so the legend goes, the many islands of Japan.

Izanagi and Izanami then created many gods and goddesses, one of whom was Amaterasu, goddess of the sun, who was born in Izanagi's left eye. Amaterasu and her husband, Susa-no-o, became the parents of more gods and goddesses, but Susa-no-o didn't get along with the others. Thrown out of heaven, he fled to earth, married a human Japanese woman, and fathered the Japanese rulers on the large island of Honshu. In the meantime, one of Amaterasu's grandsons, Ninigi, dropped down on the island of Kyushu, bringing with him a sacred

Izanagi and Izanami

bronze mirror, an iron sword, and a jeweled, claw-shaped stone as the insignia of imperial power. On Kyushu, Ninigi thus began the dynasty of gods called the sun line, in honor of his grandmother. From that sun line sprang the unbroken, divine line of emperors who have presided over Japan to this day and whose symbols remain the mirror, the sword, and the jeweled stone.

The first emperor of Japan in this legendary period was Ninigi's great-grandson, Jimmu Tenno, who ruled from 660 to 585 B.C. Jimmu, according to the legends, led the Japanese (and presumably an army of gods) out of Kyushu. Sailing to Honshu, he conquered it and built a palace in a place called Yamato, where he reigned until his death at the age of one hundred and twenty-seven years. Jimmu's god-descendants have supposedly ruled Japan ever since. Among the early rulers was the legendary empress Jengo. It is said that around 300 A.D., she gathered all the ships of her empire and invaded Korea. It was this early contact with the far more advanced civilizations of Korea, and later on China, that helped Japanese civilization grow.

Up until only a relatively short time ago — when the Emperor Hirohito denied publicly after the end of World War II that he was a god — the vast majority of Japanese believed the legends. And who are we to say that it didn't all happen that way, when so many Westerners believe in the Bible's story of Adam and Eve in the Garden of Eden? But historians look for accounts of events that are based not in mythology or divine inspiration but in well-documented facts, and they consider the history of Japan's founding colorful and charming but improbable. Even the way in which the legendary history was prepared is questionable: it was written around 700 A.D. at the bidding of a Japanese emperor. The writers wanted to impress and please their ruler and show him that Japan had a long and distinguished history like China's. What better way to do this than through mythology, with its superhuman gods and goddesses, beings with extraordinary physical strength, magical powers, and the ability to mingle with humans and share divine wisdom with them?

Very little, then, is actually known about Japan's true early history beyond the probability that a general (a human one) marched from Kyushu to Yamato and set up some sort of government around the third or fourth century A.D.; that later on Korean ambassadors traveled regularly to Japan to teach the Japanese about their great neighbor across the sea, China; and that the Japanese sent scholars, artists, and government officials many times over the years to China in search of knowledge and a new and exemplary way of life. But who were the Japanese? Where did they really come from? Historian Will Durant tells us that their origins, like all others, are "lost in the cosmic nebula of theory." He wrote that the Japanese seem to be a mixture of three groups: a yellow-skinned Mongol strain that came from or through Korea about the seventh century before Christ; a brown-black Malay and Indonesian strain that filtered in from the islands in the South Pacific; and a primitive white strain through the Ainus, who may have wandered into Japan from the region around the Amur River — which forms part of the border between China and Russia — during the Stone Age.[1] Many historians and anthropologists believe that the Ainus, who exist today in Japan as the equivalent of Native Americans, were the original settlers. One early account describes them as "strange . . . lords of the land till the Japanese came."[2] The Ainus were once a ferocious bunch of people, but they were eventually "tamed." And, like the Native Americans, their numbers were reduced by later settlers. Today there are only 20,000 or so Ainus in Japan, a handful of them full-blooded, and many of them claim that they are discriminated against by the mainstream Japanese population, and that they have the territorial rights to the islands off Hokkaido that are now in Russian hands.

Though the true origins of the Japanese are cloudy, we do know a good deal about how they grew as a people. Their growth was due in large measure to Korea and China, and to two important things the Japanese borrowed from those countries: language and religion.

Until about 400 A.D., the Japanese apparently had no written language. The ideograms — the familiar "word pictures" or pictographs they use today — were unknown. No one has yet been able to dig up any evidence of early writing, and it is hard to imagine how the Japanese got along without writing anything down. But they did, perhaps because they at least spoke a fairly sophisticated dialect. Around 360 A.D., when Koreans started visiting Japan in large numbers, they wrote down their observations in Chinese characters, and these pictographs that expressed ideas and described objects so impressed the Japanese that they borrowed them. The Japanese now had word characters that stood for the same words in Chinese, and when they didn't have a Japanese equivalent for a Chinese word, they just borrowed the Chinese word — both the pictograph and its pronunciation — and made it part of the Japanese language. That's why written Japanese has so many characters that are identical to Chinese ones (the Japanese call their pictographic characters *kanji*) and why many words the Japanese speak sound like Chinese.

Eventually, the Japanese had to refine their written language, because although they could now express the root meaning of a word, the Chinese characters they had borrowed didn't have any grammatical endings or auxiliary words — suffixes such as *-ed* and *-ish,* or words or phrases such as *could, would,* and *has been.* What the resourceful Japanese did was to create a sort of alphabet of simple letters made up of short lines, usually two or three, but no more than four. (Most of the Chinese picture characters are made up of many more brush strokes and can be incredibly complex.) They called this new system *kana* and used the new symbols along with the pictographs. Thus they were able to change a Chinese root word into one that suited Japanese grammar better and also expanded the word's meaning.

Once they had a written language, the Japanese were able to write their history, keep records, issue proclamations, set down

The pictographs for Japan *in Japanese*

laws, and compose poetry — all the things that they admired so much in the Chinese. Over the years, they continued to learn from the Chinese, and the next thing they borrowed, religion, also came from China by way of Korea. The Japanese had long practiced a religion called Shinto, or the Way of the Gods. Followers of Shinto, which is still observed today in Japan, worshiped national heroes who had been turned into gods; gods of mountains, rivers, rocks, and streams; and ancestors. Shinto had no elaborate rituals, no holy scriptures, and indeed no creed or moral code at all. Shinto shrines were (and still are) usually somber and quite plain, with gray stone lanterns and entrances marked by *torii,* high gateways made of upright wood, bronze, or granite posts, with one straight and one curved crossbeam across the top. Shinto teachers used to say that unlike "foreign devils," the Japanese did not need religious decorations and laws

The floating torii *gateway at Miyajima*

to make them good because they were naturally good, and had only to follow their own hearts. Around 550 A.D., a Korean ambassador brought over a statue of Buddha, the Indian philosopher who founded the religion of Buddhism, and copies of his sacred books. The new faith was far more elaborate than Shinto. Buddhist priests dressed in rich garments; Buddhist temples had highly polished red-and-black lacquer floors and were full of the sweet smell of incense; altars were lit with candles and decorated with flowers, bronze lanterns, silken screens, lacquered boxes containing Buddhist manuscripts, and all sorts of golden ornaments. In both substance and spirit, Buddhism far overshadowed the colder Shinto religion.

Buddhism spread slowly at first because of strong opposition from the followers of the Way of the Gods. But after about forty years, Buddhism was firmly established when the emperor, Shotoku, became a Buddhist himself and decreed it the state religion. Shotoku then began to transform Japan into almost a mirror image of China. He built gorgeous Buddhist temples everywhere and used Buddhist principles as the basis for government policies. He imported artists and skilled craftsmen from China and Korea, and he introduced a Chinese system of education, civil service, and even China's calendar; from China, the Japanese learned how to breed silkworms and weave silk, and they learned geography, medicine, and astronomy, too. Shotoku also sent numerous missions to China. Traveling five hundred miles to China across often stormy seas, eager monks, painters, poets, musicians, and government officials spent months in the Middle Kingdom (the meaning of China's name in Chinese), then returned with a wealth of knowledge that they passed on to their countrymen.

Japan became quite rich. There was an orderly government. Luxury and refinement were everywhere. Court life was full of lavish ceremonies, the arts flourished, and culture spread even to the countryside, where wealthy landowners, who were now gaining considerable influence in the country's affairs, kept stables of artists, writers, and teachers. As the years passed,

The Great Buddha at Nara

Japan found that it didn't need China's help any longer. China's input was still appreciated, but little by little, the Japanese put their own stamp on what they had learned. They created magnificent works of art that were quite distinctive from those of China and Korea. They blended buildings into the natural surroundings instead of erecting imposing structures that emphasized form alone, as the Chinese preferred. Japanese paintings featured color instead of the black ink Chinese painters used; their textiles had unique designs. The Japanese sculpted in bronze, instead of stone as the Chinese did. One of their most renowned pieces of sculpture, a gigantic Buddha completed in 749, stands to this day in Nara (Japan's first capital), near Yamato, where Jimmu Tenno reigned. It is the world's largest bronze statue, weighing four to five hundred tons and standing more than fifty feet high. As befits such a colossus, the Buddha's face is sixteen feet long and more than nine feet wide; its thumb is five-feet-three-inches long, and its mouth over three-and-a-half-feet wide. It took a quarter-ton of gold to cover its features when it was built.

But as with all golden periods, Japan's was in for trouble. As the rich got richer, the poor got poorer. The people were fed up with the extravagant ways of the palace and with the high taxes ordinary people alone had to pay. Many peasants just stopped paying taxes, moved close to wealthy landowners who could protect them, and paid them rent instead. Others left and settled in faraway areas, out of sight of the central government. Without tax money from the peasants, the government grew feebler every day. Crime increased, bandits preyed on tax collectors, and pirates began to roam the seas, plundering the ships of the wealthy. The emperors began to lose their power. Most of them were children anyway, unskilled in the ways of politics.

They were not supposed to work or even to think, because those chores were beneath them. They were also isolated from the people because these "sons of heaven" were so sacred that ordinary folk would be overwhelmed by the glorious sight of them. Not until 1872, during a period of modernization in Japan, did an emperor appear in public. When the emperor gave an audience, even to priests and noblemen, he sat behind a screen; when he walked out into his gardens, carpets were spread in front of him so that his sacred feet would not touch the earth; when he drove, it was in a covered carriage; and as he passed by, his subjects fell to their knees.

All of this made it easy for wealthy landowners to take over the real power. They allowed the emperors to exist as religious leaders and symbolic heads of the government (which was moved to Kyoto), but kept political control to themselves.

Among the powerful land-owning families during this period was one named Fujiwara. The Fujiwaras had accumulated great wealth and vast tracts of land. They were not warlike, but they managed to gain control of the government through their cunning: they provided the emperors with wives from the Fujiwara family, and they had male Fujiwaras appointed regents to govern behind the throne. This meant that an emperor's wife or mother was always a Fujiwara, and so, too, was the real ruler, the regent. So effective was this system that the Fujiwaras managed to run Japan for nearly four centuries, from about 794 to 1156 A.D.

During that period, the Fujiwaras had to fight off other powerful families and even a few emperors. Eventually a warrior class emerged. Known as samurai, they worked for the wealthy estate owners in the country and were highly skilled archers and swordsmen. Dressed in suits of armor and mounted on horses,

Samurai

they fought for their rural noblemen-bosses against rival landowners and their samurai, and eventually against the government itself. By 1185, a warrior named Yoritomo, leader of a
powerful warrior clan, the Minamoto, had defeated the rulers
in Kyoto after several years of bloody civil war. Now in charge
of the entire country, Yoritomo named a puppet emperor, or

mikado, and allowed him to remain in the capital. In 1192, Yoritomo assumed the title Sei-i-tai-shogun, which means "barbarian-subduing general-in-chief," and established a military dictatorship with headquarters at Kamakura, a city near present-day Tokyo. For the next seven hundred years, Japan would be governed by weak mikados and powerful military leaders, shoguns, some of whom were, once again, Fujiwaras. As for Yoritomo, he is still remembered with affection in Japan as a great law giver and benefactor, and the man who stopped the civil wars . . . for a time.

After Yoritomo died, plots, counterplots, and murders (some having been instigated by Yoritomo himself before his death) wiped out all of his descendants. A Fujiwara became shogun, but he was employed by a formidable master, another powerful Japanese family named Hojo. The Hojos treated the shogun just as the Fujiwaras had treated the emperors, reducing the shogun to a puppet. In that way — by ruling the shoguns who ruled the emperors — the Hojos held a firm grip on Japan from 1219 to 1333.

While such an arrangement kept Japan together, it was seen by outsiders as a sign of a weakened government. That vulnerability, along with Japan's riches, got the Chinese ruler Kublai Khan (grandson of Genghis Khan, the great Mongol conqueror of China) thinking about how he might add to his own wealth and power. At first, all Kublai thought he had to do was command the Japanese to send him gold. But his envoys to Japan were received with scorn and defiance. Not only were they refused the tribute Kublai demanded, but they were beheaded. Angered, Kublai sent an invasion force from Korea to Kyushu, but because a storm was brewing, the warriors returned home rather than risk the loss of their ships.

Kublai tried once again. In 1281, he put together a fleet of thousands of ships (Japanese historians put the number at seventy thousand) and a hundred thousand men, and sent them again to Kyushu. Kublai's fleet was, until the Allied assault on Europe in World War II, the biggest invasion force in history. But it was unsuccessful. The Japanese, anticipating a return visit from Kublai, had built an immense wall around the bay. A mighty battle between Kublai's warriors and a much smaller Japanese force raged for months, but the wall, and the smaller, faster boats of the Japanese, slowed the invaders' advance. The battle ended with the destruction of most of Kublai's soldiers. What the Japanese warriors didn't finish, a roaring typhoon that came up during the battle did. The fierce storm wrecked most of Kublai's proud fleet. The Japanese called the storm *kamikaze,* a "divine wind" sent by the gods to defend the islands of the sun. Until American troops invaded the Japanese islands of Iwo Jima and Okinawa in World War II, the engagement was the only battle the Japanese had ever fought on their own soil against foreign invaders. American sailors fighting in that war also knew the kamikaze — as the suicide pilots who flew explosive-filled planes deliberately into Allied warships in the name of the divine emperor of Japan, Hirohito.

3

Foreign Devils, Black Ships, and an American Shogun

After the Mongols' unsuccessful invasion of Japan, life returned to normal. Shoguns still ruled, emperors occasionally tried to get rid of them, feudal noblemen continued to battle one another for land, and Buddhism, commerce, and the arts flourished.

But in 1542, another kind of invasion was about to begin. The first Europeans to visit Japan, the Portuguese, with their excellent ships and superb seamanship, were on their way. The Portuguese were traders, and the first of them to reach Japan was Mendez Pinto, whose ship was wrecked on the Kyushu coast. When he and his men got ashore, they sought out the local governor, gave him a gun as a gift, and taught him how to make powder and fire the strange weapon. In six months, the Japanese made five hundred copies of the gun, and became expert marksmen. To repay Pinto, the local lord gave him permission to trade freely with the natives.[1]

Japan's privacy was now gone. Ships came and went, bringing goods from Europe to Japan and from Japan back to the

West. Soon, Catholic missionaries joined the procession, among them Saint Francis Xavier, the great Spanish Jesuit who had been active in India. Known as the Apostle of the Indies, Xavier converted thousands of Japanese from Buddhism to Catholicism. Indeed, the city of Nagasaki, target of the second atomic bomb dropped on Japan at the end of World War II, became an entirely Christian city through the labors of Xavier and his colleagues, and it was given to the Portuguese as a harbor for their ships.

At first Japan welcomed the Portuguese. Artists painted pictures of the foreign ships and sailors, and some Japanese people even wore the Western-style clothes of the Portuguese. The shoguns welcomed the traders' firearms, and guns and cannon were used in the civil wars that erupted from time to time. But then the Japanese became suspicious. For one thing, they didn't like the missionaries' intolerant attitude toward Buddhism, which was still the country's official religion, and they believed that if the country became Christian it would lose its very soul. The Japanese also felt that the missionaries and traders would be followed by foreign armies who would turn Japan into a colony.

An ambitious Japanese general, Hideyoshi, decided it was time to put a stop to the spread of Christianity and to the influence of foreigners. In 1587, he ordered all the missionaries to leave Japan. Nine monks who refused to obey were arrested, sent to Nagasaki, and crucified or burned to death; a number of Japanese converts were also executed.

A few years after that incident, the Dutch arrived in Japan. The story of Holland's relationship with Japan began, as with the Portuguese, with a shipwreck. William Adams, an English navigator with a Dutch trading fleet, washed ashore, and eventually became friends with the shogun, Iyeyasu. The shogun, who had reopened Japan to missionaries in an effort to encourage trade, gave Adams an estate and granted trading privileges to the Dutch and, later, to the English. Adams told the shogun how the Spanish Inquisition — a Catholic tribunal that hunted down and punished those who opposed Church teachings — had persecuted innocent people, and how the Protestant Dutch and English had to fight the Catholic Church's cruelty.

It was all Iyeyasu needed to hear. Whether it was the Dutch influence that made him take action, or whether he had already made up his mind that Christianity was not for his people, is hard to say. Iyeyasu reacted sternly, and his policies were carried through even more harshly by his son Hidetada after Iyeyasu's death in 1616. Christian monks were once again expelled from the country, and their churches destroyed. Japanese converts were ordered to renounce the new faith. When some of the monks and converts refused to go along with Hidetada's orders, he took stronger measures. There were mass executions of missionaries and Japanese Christians. Crucifixes were sent to the villages and everyone, even children, was ordered to trample on them or die. In 1637, the embattled Christians made one last attempt to defy the government. Some forty thousand of them fled to a strong fort in Kyushu, where they held out for several months against government forces. Dutch traders helped the Japanese attackers, but they claimed later they didn't know the people inside the fort were Christians. In April 1638, the castle was overrun, and everyone inside was killed.

It was the end of Christianity in Japan, and it was also the end of Japan's contact with the outside world — for a time. Except for some trade with the Dutch and the Chinese — who

were allowed to use one port, a small island near Nagasaki —
no foreigner was permitted entry into Japan. Japanese citizens
could not travel abroad, and if they tried, they would be executed. Japanese sailors who had left were not allowed to return.
This state of affairs would last for over two hundred years.
Essentially isolated from the rest of the world, Japan went its
own way fairly successfully, developing its industries and paying more attention to its own culture. Some writers say the
Japanese economy stagnated during this period; others say it
was a period of growth. No matter which was true, Japan
became more Japanese, and it was not until the four black-
hulled ships of an American naval officer, Commodore Matthew Perry, steamed into Yedo Bay (now Tokyo Bay) in 1853
that Japan would be forced to accept foreigners and their ways
once again.

Perry's voyage to Japan was the U.S. government's idea. For
months, America, Great Britain, and Russia had been trying to
convince Japan to restore foreign trade, but the Japanese weren't
interested. The U.S. also wanted coaling stations in Japan
where American ships could stop on their way to San Francisco
to trade with China. Japan's rejection of all the offers began to
grate on the West, which could not understand how any nation
could shut itself off so tightly.

As so often happens when countries won't do what other
countries want them to do, there was widespread talk of using
force to settle the issue. As one American diplomat put it at the
time, "If she doesn't open her ports, we will open our ports."
"Our ports" meant the gun ports on warships.[2]

Commodore Perry's ships, anchored in Yedo Bay, did not use
their guns, although there is little doubt that if Perry's request

for a meeting with representatives of the emperor had been refused, he would have used force. If he had, the Japanese would have been no match for the American ships.

Aware of the Japanese's appreciation of beauty, the U.S. president, Millard Fillmore, had his letter to the emperor — which requested free trade, a fueling station, and friendship — placed inside a box of pure gold that was then encased in a rosewood box with gold hinges. The Japanese accepted the box, acknowledged its contents, and stalled as long as they dared. They asked Perry to return home and wait for a formal reply. Perry said he'd wait, but not at home. Promising to return to Japan in a few months, he sailed for Hong Kong. While there, he received word from the Dutch that the emperor had died, and that it would be better if the Americans went home and forgot about going back to Japan.

It was a ruse. The shogun, not the emperor, had died. In February 1854, Perry's fleet returned to Japan. This time it included seven ships — three frigates and four sloops-of-war. The display was enough to convince the Japanese that they had no choice but to sign the trade treaty. Quickly, other nations took advantage of the break, and soon Japan's doors were opened wide.

Although the U.S. treaty was forced on Japan, in the long run it would benefit the country by helping it to modernize and become more powerful. Perry himself had gotten the Japanese off to a good start in that direction: among the "gifts" he presented the Japanese were a locomotive and several miles of track; a long length of telegraph wire and the instruments for sending and receiving messages; guns, clocks, sewing machines, charts, and maps.

Japan now entered a period of Westernization. The ban on

Christianity was lifted, and missionaries returned. The shoguns were still in power, but soon the emperor's authority would be restored, at least on paper. This happened in 1867, a year that marked the beginning of what the Japanese call the Meiji Restoration of Enlightened Rule. The emperor at the time was only fourteen, and although he was supposed to be in charge, it was really the samurai and nobles who were. This time, though, the rulers were more reform-minded, and they abolished the old feudal system and replaced it with a system of government borrowed from the West. Over the years, the samurai were stripped of their swords; merchant families and business cartels acquired more power; and a constitution and a legislature were established. Shinto, the Way of the Gods, was made the official state religion because it reflected the god-emperor's traditional and religious authority. "The emperor rules the land and people in accordance with the oracle of Amaterasu, the imperial ancestor," the country's leaders decreed. "The fundamental principle of national rule lies in the people's revering the oracle and endeavoring to expand the great way of *kami*, the gods."[3]

Gaslights were installed in the streets, followed later by electric light bulbs; railroads and telegraph lines linked parts of the country; Japanese emissaries visited the United States and Europe; a powerful naval fleet was built. A student of the West, Japan would learn its lessons well, and soon would no longer be just a quaint Asian coaling station and trading stop for foreign visitors. The Land of the Rising Sun, whose emperor and shoguns had been humiliated by Commodore Perry's menacing black gunboats, would in the very near future be a formidable force in world affairs.

From the Emperor Meiji's time to the present, events in Japan moved with seemingly lightning speed. There were revolts and rebellions, and wars against foreign powers. The Japanese fought China over control of Korea in 1894, won, and began a period of expansion in Asia. A few years later, from 1904 to 1905, Japan fought and defeated Russia in another war over bordering territories, the first time an Asian power had defeated a European one. By the time Emperor Hirohito ascended to the throne in 1926 — his reign would be the longest in the history of his two-thousand-year-old dynasty — Japan had occupied Korea and several Pacific islands, as well as Manchuria, Taiwan, and other parts of China.

In 1941, military men led by General Hideki Tojo gained complete control of the government, just as the warrior class had done during the Fujiwara period hundreds of years before. With Hirohito a puppet emperor on the throne, Tojo became prime minister of Japan, and it was he who helped mount the Japanese attack on December 7, 1941, which destroyed the American fleet berthed at Pearl Harbor, Hawaii, and brought America into World War II. The Japanese, whose aggressive policies had gotten them into a war with China in 1937, were intent on expanding their influence in Asia. They reckoned that the American people could not stomach a long and costly war, and that by destroying the U.S. fleet in Hawaii they would have a clear path to conquering the islands in the South Pacific. At the beginning, Japan, which had formed an alliance with Germany and Italy known as the Axis, won a great many victories. Japan conquered Singapore, the Philippines, Burma, Malaysia, the Dutch East Indies, and many other territories in the Pacific region.

But by 1945, the United States, Britain, China, and the other Allied powers proved too much for the Japanese Imperial Army and Navy. Little by little, the Allies regained the territory captured by the Japanese. Japanese home islands were invaded for the first time since Kublai Khan had sent his fleet there in 1281, and Japan's major cities were burned to the ground by the firebombs dropped by Allied warplanes. Although defeated, Japan's military government refused to quit. On August 6 and 9, 1945, United States planes dropped history's first atomic bombs on Hiroshima and Nagasaki, killing more than a hundred thousand people and leaving hundreds of thousands more poisoned by deadly radiation. A week later, Japan surrendered unconditionally. In Tokyo, hundreds of patriotic Japanese men and women killed themselves on the grounds of the emperor's palace as an apology to their god-king for having lost the war.

Soon after, Japan was occupied by a foreign army for the first time in its long history. The war had cost the country some three million dead, and the loss of countless homes and industries. Japan's economy was in ruins. U.S. soldiers, under the command of General Douglas MacArthur — who became the Supreme Commander for the Allied Powers — took over almost every aspect of the country's life. Japan's weapons factories were dismantled, its armed forces were broken up, and its businesses and government — from banks to civil service offices — were put under control of the occupation. Tojo was executed as a war criminal, and Americans in uniform became familiar sights all through Japan. During the period of the occupation, which lasted from 1945 to 1952, Emperor Hirohito was allowed to retain the throne, but only as a symbol, as his ancestors had been for centuries. For many Japanese, MacArthur was both god and shogun. Once again, it appeared that Japan had a military dictator.

But there was a major difference. Though Japan was occupied by American soldiers under the command of a general, the U.S. occupation of Japan was unlike any other in history. "We thought the soldiers would mistreat us, but they gave us milk" was how some Japanese civilians put it. Indeed, the period was notable for how well the Japanese were treated by the occupying forces. Instead of punishing a conquered people, the Americans instituted reforms and set up a democratic form of government that allowed the Japanese to govern themselves. A new constitution that restored or instituted many civil rights was written. It renounced war, and it established equality between the sexes.

The constitution also, as mentioned, took away the emperor's political power but allowed him and his successors to occupy the palace as a figurehead, preside at ceremonial functions, and

MacArthur and Hirohito

receive visiting heads of state. In his memoirs, General Mac-Arthur told an interesting story about Emperor Hirohito, one that says a good deal about the emperor as a human being. A month after the Japanese surrendered aboard the U.S. battleship *Missouri,* Hirohito showed up at the U.S. embassy in Tokyo for an audience with MacArthur. The emperor was dressed in a formal morning coat and a top hat. The general offered him a cigarette, and although Hirohito never smoked, he accepted it. MacArthur thought that the emperor, fearing that he was to meet the same fate as Tojo, was there to plead for his life. Instead, Hirohito told him that he had come to "bear sole responsibility for every political and military decision made and action taken by my people in the conduct of the war." He could have been executed for making such a statement. MacArthur wrote that he was "moved to the very marrow of my bones," adding, "He was an emperor by inherent birth, but in that instant I knew I faced the First Gentleman of Japan in his own right."[4]

Later, Hirohito made another announcement that stunned his people and shook the foundations of a belief system that had existed for centuries. In 1946, during his annual New Year's message to his country, he said this:

"The bonds between Us and Our countrymen do not have their basis in the fictitious idea that the emperor is manifest god." With that brief sentence, Hirohito put an end to a myth.[5] *for many people*

Part Two

Modern Japanese Society

4

Beliefs and Customs

Hirohito died in 1989, and his son, Akihito, is the new emperor. His position remains a symbolic one, as it has been for many centuries. But, unlike his predecessors, Akihito has traveled extensively and enjoys a somewhat freer life. Well educated, his interest is marine biology, as was his father's, and he is a specialist in fish tumors.

Still, he can never forget his position, nor the traditions and formalities of his country's rich past. When he was thirteen years old, his American teacher asked members of his class what each wanted to be when they grew up. The then crown prince replied solemnly, "I shall be the emperor." A few years later, he was decorated by his father with the Grand Cordon of the Supreme Order of the Chrysanthemum and with the First Class Order of the Rising Sun with Pawlonia Flowers. This in a country with two houses of parliament that function much like our congress, as well as a prime minister and a cabinet.

Thus, the ancient customs, honors, and beliefs persist in modern-day Japan. While it is doubtful that Japan will ever see a return to imperial power, one can be certain that it will never lose touch with its colorful past. Japanese society today offers many examples of that link. You can see it in the religion and the language, in the proverbs, the food, and the many ceremonies. The tea ceremony is probably the best known of these to Westerners. Known in Japanese as *chanoyu,* it was introduced by Zen monks, first as a way to help them to meditate. Later, it became an elaborate ritual with all sorts of beautiful and delicate utensils. The women servers, with their graceful movements, have become a symbol of sophistication, and, indeed, training in the ceremony has long been part of the cultivated woman's education.

In much of what they do, the Japanese are today what they were many centuries ago. Their religion is one important example. The dominant faiths are still Shinto and Buddhism, and fewer than a million Japanese are Christians. Japanese are still married in an old Shinto ceremony but buried with Buddhist rites; a new house is blessed by a Shinto priest, after which the owner goes to a Buddhist temple to pray for the money to pay for it. Japanese homes still have small shrines with pictures of the deceased to keep their memory alive. (Contrary to what some Westerners believe, the Japanese do not worship their ancestors with these shrines; they simply honor their memories.)

Freedom of religion is guaranteed in Japan, as it is in America, but the Japanese, as throughout most of their history, are not especially religious. Still, there are plenty of ancient religious symbols everywhere — temples, shrines, altars, stone images of the Buddha and Shinto gods — and many different religious ceremonies. And, as in the past, religious observances are confined to events like marriages, births, and funerals, along with visits to sacred places during certain holidays, such as New Year's Eve, and the coming of spring and autumn.

Another important way to understand the beliefs and customs of any people is through their proverbs and superstitions. Proverbs, those popular sayings that compress a lot of wisdom (or sometimes ignorance, superstition, and prejudice) into a very few, well-chosen words, are common to virtually every nation on earth. Proverbs spring from the minds and hearts of the people, and thus are a reflection of their unique ideas and beliefs. By examining these means of expression, we can often see the differences and similarities between our culture and that of another country. Japan has a lot of proverbs, just as we do, and they are an important part of the country's rich cultural heritage. Many Japanese proverbs have close or exact counterparts in English, others none whatsoever. We'll leave it to you to come up with English equivalents to some of the following selections, and to interpret a few others.

- Spilled water never returns to the tray.
- Obey the customs of the place you are visiting.
- Man is as old as he feels, and a woman is as old as she looks.
- Man imitates; woman follows.
- A man cannot be known by his looks alone.
- Among carp, carp is king.
- The early riser has seven gains.
- Tomorrow blows another wind.
- The game is not worth the candle.
- Dust piled makes a mountain.
- In haste, one travels in a circle.
- Have an umbrella ready before it rains.

- An able hawk hides its claws.
- A child may grow and prosper, even though he is an orphan.
- "No, thank you" has lost many a good butter-cake.
- Patience is a remedy for every sorrow, and patient men win the day.
- There are more ways to kill a dog than by hanging.
- They must hunger in frost that will not work in heat.
- Hard words break no bones.
- Train an untamed horse by facing it head–on.
- Good blood cannot lie.
- The nail that sticks out is the one that gets hammered down.
- Fireworks with elaborate names are all just smoke.
- When you draw a horse, forget the coat or you'll end up with something else.
- When we wish to be dutiful to our parents, they are no more.
- Look at the congregation before you preach.
- Glasses and lasses are brittle wares.
- One of these days is none of these days.
- A naked man never lost anything.
- Do not put the thief in charge of the key.
- Those who live must die; those who meet must part.
- The weed and the dandelion do not envy the rose or the lily.
- When the head moves, so, too, will the tail.
- Catch the rabbit before you cook it.
- Even weeds have their day.
- No one laughs from the beginning of the year to the end.
- A smiling boy seldom proves a good servant.

- He that will not endure labor in this world, let him not be born.
- An idle brain is the devil's shop.
- It is a shame to steal, but worse to carry home.
- Feel your parents' minds in your bones.
- Too much pudding chokes a dog.[1]

Many Japanese beliefs and practices rely heavily on chance, or even magic. The Japanese have their superstitions, just as we do. They go to fortune-tellers, analyze dreams, and follow horoscopes. According to the Japanese zodiac system, each year is ruled by one of twelve animals: the snake, boar, rat, and others. The ruling animal of the year in which one is born, for example, determines whether one is charming, wise, handsome, beautiful, fussy, lazy, and so on. Snake people, for instance, are supposedly quiet, bright, and incredibly fortunate. Rats are charming, but tend to be miserly; boars are chivalrous and don't make many friends, but when they do are loyal for life.

Not a few Japanese let the zodiac govern their lives. On the basis of a certain year, they might choose a mate, enter into a business arrangement with a compatible colleague, or pick their friends. In the Year of the Fiery Horse, for instance, many Japanese avoid marriages because a woman married under that sign is supposedly apt to murder her husband!

Just as we avoid the number thirteen because it is supposed to bring bad luck and accidents, the Japanese shun the number four, because the word for it, *shi,* can also mean death; and the number nine, the word for which can also mean pain. It is not uncommon for hospital and hotel rooms to skip those numbers on doors.

Japanese men often carry fans, but not for the same reason

women do, that is, as a symbol of feminine shyness or coyness. When a man has a fan, he might use it to cool himself, but he's also reminding himself of the ancient samurai, who carried fans along with their swords. Women have their reminders, too. When a Japanese woman is married in a traditional ceremony, she might wear a headband — to cover up the horns of jealousy that she is allegedly born with.

The Japanese also watch for many omens while going about their daily lives. Here are a few:

- If the first person you meet when you leave your home is a woman, you'll have a good day; if it's a Buddhist priest, you'll have a bad day.
- If a snake crosses the road in front of you from right to left, you'll come into some money.
- If you hit your chopsticks against your rice bowl, you'll be poor.
- If a funeral procession overtakes you, watch out!
- When your ear itches, you'll get good news; when your nose itches, there'll be a birth in a family you know.
- Sneeze three times and it means someone loves you; sneeze four times and you've got a cold.
- If you dream of a moonlit sky, you'll rise in position and become famous.
- If you dream you are a handsome man or a lovely woman, it's a sign of bad luck.
- Dream of ice and you'll be married.[2]

Japanese customs and beliefs even show up in some of the things they have borrowed from America. Baseball, or *besuboru*, as it's known over there, is a good example. The Japanese fell in love with the game when it was introduced to them in 1873. The first professional teams were established in Japan in 1936 after American stars such as Babe Ruth and Lou Gehrig visited.

Japanese baseball is played by the same rules as in the U.S., but the Japanese have put their own stamp on the game. For instance, Japanese culture frowns on emotional outbursts, and arguments, so common in our big leagues, are rare; no real team player would ever act belligerently. Managers are taskmasters, but they are also fathers, counselors, and even matchmakers when a player has gone too long without a wife. And when a team is doing poorly, the players and managers apologize — profusely. In his delightful book *The Chrysanthemum and the Bat,* Robert Whiting gives a few examples of some things a humbled team manager might say:

> *On losing seven games in a row:* "*I apologize to the fans for this disgrace. I just hope it will get better. I don't know what has come over my pitching staff. They have lost their fighting spirit.*"
>
> *On being in last place:* "*This cannot continue. . . . No matter how low we sink we must strengthen our resolve and play to the utmost of our ability for the rest of the season . . . I will hold a meeting to discuss the matter with* [*the team*]. *My humble apologies.*"

Players, too, know the meaning of repentance. "I am sorry," said a pitcher after a disappointing loss. "I wanted to throw my curveball, but they were aiming for it, so I had to go with my *shuto boru* [screwball]. Unluckily, my *shuto* was too sweet, and they hit me. I will do my best to redeem myself."[3]

5

Japanese Home Life

Baseball, proverbs, and superstitions are, as we have seen, important to our understanding of Japanese culture. Home life, too, is a reflection of that culture, as it is of any country's. Consider young Hiroshi Miyawaki and his sister, Atsuko. When they came to the United States with their parents — their father had been transferred here by his jewelry firm in Japan — the teenagers were awed by the large house they would occupy for the next three years. Located in Westchester County, a New York suburb, it had a half-acre of land around it, a two-car garage, four bedrooms, a family room, a living room, a dining room, a spacious attic, and a kitchen so large that, as Atsuko put it, her whole family "could actually eat and hang out in it at the same time."

The kids not only had their own spacious rooms, but they and their parents could have friends stay over for the night or the weekend. "I couldn't believe it that we even had two pullout sofas in the sitting rooms if we had a crowd," Hiroshi said, laughing. "Only in America, right?"

Nearby were schools, a hospital, a variety of restaurants, a pond, a public park, churches, gas stations, two shopping malls, a golf course, a bowling alley, and a riding stable. "Before we left, I joked to my family that maybe in the U.S.A. we would live like the emperor," Hiroshi's father said. "To some, how we're living might seem like that."

What the Miyawakis had left behind in Tokyo, Japan's most populous city, was quite different. They had lived on the fourth floor of a six-story "mansion" (*mansion* being the Japanese word for an apartment building), which hardly resembled our definition of a mansion. More than 75 percent of Japanese live in cities — in apartments or small row houses. Most of the buildings, like the one the Miyawakis occupied, were built after World War II to replace the ones destroyed when U.S. planes firebombed and leveled the large cities. The Miyawakis' mansion was boxlike and made of drab gray concrete. There was a small, fence-enclosed courtyard that contained a tiny garden surrounded by asphalt. A few benches around the edge of the yard, three trees, a slide, and some swings were the only extras.

The apartment itself consisted roughly of one rectangular space that could be divided into rooms by sliding screens, called shoji. By moving the screens, the Miyawakis made three sleeping rooms with mat floors and futons, thick cotton mattresses that had to be aired out each day, folded, and put away in a small closet when the family got up. Another screen blocked off the living room, which contained the TV, a pair of small lounge chairs, a bookcase, a tea table, stereo equipment, records, and tapes. There were no sofas, rocking chairs, or end tables. Because the Japanese consider shoes to be unclean, the Miyawakis always removed them when they entered the spotless apartment, exchanging them for slippers arranged in a neat row just inside the door.

The Miyawakis, unlike many other Japanese families their size, had an eat-in kitchen, but it was far smaller than the one they had in New York. The table and four chairs had to compete for space with a sink, a small refrigerator, an equally small washing machine light enough to be pushed around on its wheels (clothes were hung out to dry on the narrow balcony), an ironing board, a vacuum cleaner, and a few cabinets. The bathroom and its fixtures were also small: a washbowl "the size of an LP record album," a plastic toilet and plastic bathtub that would have fit easily into a child's playhouse, and a compact hand-shower. The kitchen and bathroom were the only rooms with floors not covered with straw mats.

Other Japanese in the same building lived in even smaller quarters, and ate not in a kitchen but seated on pillows around a low table on the floor of the living room. "We really didn't need much else, though," Atsuko recalled. "We even had the three C's — car, conditioner [meaning air-conditioner], and color TV, just like other Japanese families. It was just the space. But we got used to it, since we really didn't know much else, unless we visited this one friend of my dad's who had a big place, or roamed around in a hotel."

Even that friend's home couldn't compare to many of our homes. It was a small, two-family concrete building so close to the others on the street that they all could have been part of an apartment complex. Given the lack of available land around Tokyo and the astronomical prices one has to pay if suitable land can be found, it was no wonder that the Miyawakis, like so many other Japanese, found that owning a house, small though it might be, was just a dream. "But we were lucky in

that my dad was able to live in Tokyo," said Hiroshi. "Many of the dads have to live far out, where it's cheaper, and getting into the city takes a long time." The Miyawakis did own their apartment, but only, like most Japanese families, with the help of an expensive bank housing loan.

In Westchester, Hiroshi and Atsuko got used to "eating Western" quite often, even at home — including burgers and hot dogs, pizza and burritos. While they had visited American fast-food restaurants in Tokyo, they hadn't done so often, and their diet at home was certainly not as heavy as that in many U.S. homes. Japanese families eat far less red meat and dairy products than we do, and far more fish, vegetables, and cereals than we do. "My mom figures we're all going to kill ourselves over here," said Atsuko. "But it's really hard to resist. There's so much meat and those other things, and they give you so much in the restaurants. My dad brought home a picture he took of a steak that he had at a company dinner, and we thought it was for four people."

The Miyawakis would probably be better off sticking to their traditional diet — small portions of seafood and vegetables, with hardly any fat — because Japan's death rate from heart disease is lower than that in other industrialized countries. There is concern these days that as more and more Japanese teens favor a Western-style diet over the lighter, traditional foods, they will start to feel the effects. Already, Japan's elementary and junior high school kids have grown taller and gained more weight than the previous generations.

The physical changes began as Japan recovered from World War II. Nutrition not only improved markedly from meager, vitamin-deficient diets to plenty of healthy food, but Western foods — meat, bread, and rich desserts — became more popular. The gradual switch from kneeling on floors to sitting in chairs, again Western-style, is another explanation doctors give for the longer, unbowed legs now so commonplace in Japan. But Japanese doctors are also starting to see higher levels of cholesterol — the artery-clogging substance that contributes to heart attacks — in the blood of young adults. Moreover, many Japanese teens smoke cigarettes, and more older Japanese are dying from lung cancer these days than in the past.

In Tokyo, Atsuko and Hiroshi's grandparents did not live with them. They lived in their own homes, not far away, and the Miyawakis visited them often. This arrangement is not unusual in modern Japan. Although Japanese families have long cared for their elderly members, the situation is changing, and the number of parents living with their adult children is declining. Some of the reasons are working conditions that require major moves, as was the case with Mr. Miyawaki; the growth of dual-career families; and friction between young married couples, many of whom are nontraditional, and their elderly parents who cling to traditional life-styles. In 1960, the proportion of people over sixty-five who were living with their children or other relatives was nearly 90 percent, far higher than in other advanced nations. Today, around 45 percent of the elderly live with their children; the rest live with their spouses, alone, or in houses for the elderly.

The role of grandparents in rearing the grandchildren has changed, too. If Atsuko and Hiroshi had been born years earlier, chances are they would have been raised far more strictly. At one time, the so-called *ie,* or ancestral, system governed the family. This meant that the household line was carried on by the eldest son, and he had to stay at home with his parents even after marriage. Quite often, two or even three generations of husbands and wives lived together in the same house.

Under the *ie* system, individual family members kept their personal wishes to themselves for the sake of the family. Children were guided more by their grandmothers than their mothers, and the mother often had no voice at all in bringing them up. After World War II, the traditional system was wiped away (although it still exists in the minds and hearts of the elderly) by the new constitution, which called for respect for individual dignity and equality of the sexes. While some Japanese families still stick to the old *ie* concept, the older people who try to exert influence on the children often don't have much luck these days, and most Japanese teenagers are being brought up by parents raised after the war.[1]

But even though Hiroshi and Atsuko were not brought up in the *ie* tradition, their parents did, nonetheless, raise them to respect Japanese traditions and culture — blending Japanese values into modern-day life — as do most young Japanese parents today. They were taught to have great respect for their grandparents and for their schoolteachers. Since their mother did not work outside of the home, she spent a good deal of time taking care of household needs and making sure that her children studied hard. Like most Japanese teenagers, Atsuko and Hiroshi wore uniforms to school, joined various clubs that gave them not only companions but taught them the meaning of group harmony, and followed strict rules of etiquette.

"We had to be home at certain hours," said Hiroshi. "We ate together when we could, we were taught to be quiet in the presence of older people, and we could never do things to our uniforms that would make them stand out." Atsuko recalled that her mom reprimanded her because she changed her hairstyle one morning when she went off to school, something that neither her mother nor the school authorities could accept.

Other moms in Japan, as we will see in the next chapter, follow a different path, working either full- or part-time to earn enough money to support the family. Sometimes in such households the kids are left on their own much of the time, and the arrangement more often than not works out well, the kids being none the worse for having a working mother. Other times, just as in the U.S., the kids are unable to handle the freedom; it can be particularly difficult for Japanese kids since their traditional culture doesn't support that kind of freedom. As we will see later, some rebel, create problems for themselves and their families, and even drop out of school. It would be wrong to suggest, however, that this sort of un-Japanese family behavior happens only when two parents are working. Even moms who are home all the time have their hands full. Sometimes the mother is so obsessed with the children's education that she indulges them, buying anything they want if they'll just keep their grades up. Other moms are so caught up in maintaining Japanese tradition that they become too strict, something that doesn't sit well with modern teens in Japan. These kids, too, rebel.

"What it all amounts to," said Mrs. Miyawaki,

is finding the middle road between the old and the new. That is most hard for a Japanese parent to do, especially one who has elderly parents brought up in the old ways and who believe that too much individuality is a bad thing. When we return to Japan, as we must, our kids will be back in Japanese schools, mostly with students who have never traveled, and it will take them time to readjust, but they must do that for it is our home. My parents couldn't understand this move, and told us that it would ruin the kids. It's sad they refuse to visit us here, but that is their way. I tell them we're a new kind of family, that times and ideas change, even in Japan. We'll just have to see if it's for the better.

6

Sex and Sex Roles in Japan

Mrs. Miyawaki was right when she said that times and ideas change. But in a rigid culture like Japan's, change comes slowly, and it is often feared. As a Japanese proverb puts it, "In haste, one travels in a circle." One important area in which change has come but not as quickly as some would like it is the attitude of men toward women in Japan. Consider this example of women's traditional role:

Many years ago, in the city of Kyoto, workmen were building a new Buddhist temple. Heaped inside were coils of rope, each as long and as thick as a ship's cable. But the rope was not designed for use at sea, and it was not made of the usual hemp. The coils were woven of women's hair, each strand carefully twisted and spliced and ready to be used for hoisting beams and tiles in the construction of the temple. The hair was donated by thousands of women who answered the call for contributions to the new temple and who had nothing else to give. One rope was 250 feet long, the gift of 3,500 women from one province alone.

One visitor to Japan during the temple construction wrote:

When one recollects the pride which Japanese women take in their abundant hair, the care they show in its arrangement, and the entire absence in Japan of hats or bonnets to conceal the sacrifice, their action is remarkable. And when we perceived among the usual black strands occasional streaks of white and gray, proving that this enthusiasm extended from youth to age, it seemed to us a most touching proof of popular devotion to a sacred cause that we had ever seen.[1]

The writer did not say it, but the hair donations represented more than devotion to Buddhism. They were one example of the many sacrifices that Japanese women have made over the centuries.

Traditionally, Japanese women have been passive, obedient, and subservient to the men in their lives. In the home, they were responsible for the education and care of the children and for the household chores. Seen but rarely heard, they had few rights. For years, Japanese women about to be married had to shave their eyebrows, pluck their lashes, and stain their teeth jet-black — the object being to make them hideous to other men. Married men could have many mistresses, but a woman caught committing adultery could be killed. Husbands could divorce their wives easily, even for talking too much. As another proverb warned, "A woman with a three-inch tongue can kill a man six feet tall." Shoguns often handed over female relatives to the enemy as hostages or to wealthy families as gifts. Female servants had to bow before their masters, their heads touching the floor; when serving tea, they had to approach on their knees. Some Buddhist sects taught that women were sinful and could only be saved when they were reborn as men. Even the mythical goddess, Izanami, was treated badly by the early myth writers: she was blamed for the birth of a deformed child, and when she was married to the god Izanagi, she made the mistake of speaking first, and the marriage ritual had to be done all over again to allow her god-husband to dominate the ceremony.[2]

There were, of course, exceptions. Upper-class women were well educated and some wrote highly acclaimed novels. Many of them inherited property, something lower-class women could not do, and several females ruled as empresses and even fought as warriors. In general, though, Japanese women have not had an easy time of it. Even today, when their situation has improved somewhat, old perceptions die hard, and many people still fail to understand or accept the Japanese woman's newer role in society.

Some of us still see Madame Butterfly when we think of Japanese women. She was the graceful kimono-clad heroine of the opera of the same name by Giacomo Puccini. Betrothed to an American naval officer who returns to the United States, she kills herself when her husband-to-be comes back to Japan married to an American woman. Poor Butterfly was too disgraced by the affair to live a normal life in Japan, and so she stabbed herself — and at the same time reinforced the West's view of the dutiful Japanese woman.

There are still many Madame Butterflys in Japan. Young and old, they are docile and doll-like, giggly and charming, and eager to please — primarily to please men. When I lived in Japan, there was a woman secretary in our office who always insisted, when we left together, that I go out the door first, and she held the umbrella over my head if it was raining. She made tea and served it to me in the office, bowed deeply each time I showed up, and refused to call me by my first name.

Her behavior was, of course, culturally determined. But it does demonstrate the wide difference between the way Western women and many Japanese women respond to men. Traditional women (and men) will always be part of any country's population, and there is nothing wrong with that. Even though some people feel that tradition can be stifling, "it does not mean that the living are dead," as English prime minister Harold Mac-Millan once said; "it means that the dead are living."

However, too much tradition can get in the way of progress. Insofar as Japanese women are concerned, it could be said that the emphasis on tradition has probably hindered them more than it has helped them. In all fairness, we should point out that many Japanese men have changed in the way they behave toward women. A recent survey by the prime minister's office noted that 60 percent of fathers in their twenties said raising kids made their lives worthwhile and that they were willing to share parenting and other duties. There are also any number of Japanese men who do not fit the old stereotype of the man who orders his wife around like a servant. This is especially true in dual-career households, where the wife sometimes has the more important job.

What are Japanese women really like today?

The first thing to remember is that they are still Japanese, culturally and in their general beliefs and behavior, just as Japanese men are. But they also want the same things that many Western women want: marriage and families, a say in controlling their bodies, and opportunities to learn, work, and run for public office. Mariko Sugahara Bando, a Japanese woman writer who specializes in issues involving women and the elderly, points out that the image Westerners have of Japanese women — an image that encompasses kimonos, tea ceremonies, flower arranging, and self-sacrifice for husband and children — is an accurate picture of traditional attributes to be sure, but they are also fragmentary aspects of modern Japanese womanhood.

"The socio-economic changes in present-day Japan have greatly altered the lives of women," she writes.

> *Of course, compared with men on the whole, women still spend more time and energy doing the traditional female activities of housekeeping and taking care of the children. . . . At the same time, it is true that the days when getting married, having children, doing housework, and bringing up children were considered the natural calling for women have slipped into the past. . . . Today, women in increasing numbers are taking advantage of education to develop abilities and awareness in no way inferior to those of men. With the rapid growth of the economy, companies have come to employ many women, including housewives. And although these women are often at the bottom of the company ladder, they nonetheless are gaining the experience of having their time and labor converted to money.*[3]

Most of us probably don't realize it, but Japanese women have long wanted equality with men. It's just that given the stern rules of their society, they couldn't always express their feelings. They might have descended from the sun goddess but, as a Japanese feminist, Raicho Hiratsuka, said many years ago, they were reduced to mere reflections of others, like the moon.

Occasionally, Japanese women did speak out, and sometimes their government acted favorably (albeit often grudgingly) to help them. In the 1800s and early 1900s, for instance, slaves and prostitutes were freed, women were allowed to marry non-Japanese men, women won the right to bring action for divorce, women workers struck at factories, the Tokyo Women's Medical School was founded, Tokyo University admitted women for the first time, housewives demonstrated against rising rice prices and touched off a series of riots, women teachers were able to get time off before and after childbirth, late-night hours for women textile workers were abolished, and women were allowed to take the bar examination to become lawyers. In 1945, for the first time in Japan's history, women were allowed to vote. The change was apparently made because some Japanese knew the U.S. occupation forces planned to institute equal voting rights for women and they wanted credit to go to the Japanese government. General MacArthur reportedly told the prime minister that the granting of voting rights to women "has been the only good policy put into effect by the Japanese government."[4]

More reforms came during the occupation, notably under the new constitution, which clearly stated: "All of the people are equal under the law and there shall be no discrimination in political, economic or social relations because of race, creed, sex, social status or family origin." New laws allowed adults to marry without having to obtain the consent of their parents; women could now inherit property, and parental power, traditionally in the hands of the father, was given jointly to father and mother.

Today, some 25 million women are working in Japan, representing about 40 percent of the work force; at the end of World War II, about 13 million were working. More than 95 percent of all girls go to high school, and 38 percent to universities or junior colleges (the figures are slightly higher than those for boys); in 1930, only 13 percent of the female secondary school–age population was in school, and in 1950 only 37 percent went to high school. As more and more women in Japan have taken charge of their lives, the birth rate has gone down: before the war, the average number of children per family was five; now the average family has two.[5]

In politics, too, Japanese women have begun to make themselves heard. While they hold only 4 percent of the seats in the Diet, the country's legislature, the number of female lawmakers is expected to grow over the years, perhaps because the number of eligible women voters now surpasses that of men by three million. The head of one of the nation's leading opposition parties, the Socialist Party, is a woman, Takako Doi; women have also been appointed to cabinet posts and serve as judges and public prosecutors.

Japanese women also make headlines in sports and various adventurous pursuits: Midori Ito, age twenty-two, won the silver medal for Olympic figure skating in 1992, making her the nation's first medalist in that competition; volleyball champion Motoko Ohbayashi, twenty-four, at six foot, one inch, destroys the stereotype of the demure Japanese woman; and, also in 1992, against the strong protests of her mother, Kyoko Imakiire, twenty-seven, became the first Japanese woman to

Midori Ito

sail single-handedly nonstop around the world, a journey of more than 33,000 miles that took her nine months.

But even though Japanese women are moving to a new beat, and though the kimono has been largely replaced by designer clothes and American jeans, they have a way to go yet to match the achievements of women in the West. Women are technically equal under Japanese law, but reality doesn't always match the law.

Take marriage customs, for example. While young adults can meet mates and wed without parental consent, it's not always a great idea. If the young couple's family is not involved in the match, married life gets off to a rocky start. Most marriages in Japan are still arranged by families and friends. A young woman who "just falls in love" with someone she's met somewhere has a hard time fitting in if she pursues the relationship to marriage. Also, it's important in Japan for a woman to marry before she reaches thirty (around twenty-five is considered the ideal age). It's true that an increasing number of women are postponing marriage in favor of a career, but still, if a woman doesn't marry on society's schedule, chances are people will start talking about her, wondering what her problem is, perhaps criticizing her because she chose to wait on marriage while she paid more attention to becoming someone and making money. Life can be very difficult for a young Japanese woman who does not go along with society's flow.

And after a woman is married, unless her husband is one of the rare "liberated" Japanese men, she will be expected to devote herself full-time to the household chores and caring for the children. Married women in Japan do have more spare time today than their grandmothers did, but they are rarely invited to accompany their husband to social functions connected with his work, and they have to accept his after-hours meetings and visits to restaurants and bars, and perhaps even ignore his flirtations with hostesses and waitresses. Married people may love each other, but the notion of separate lives is still deeply set in

Japanese society. Man is the breadwinner, woman the home-maker, and while this sort of role playing is changing, it has not yet changed enough to make a major difference in the lives of most Japanese. Women may be working outside the home, but they're still paid less than men, are not often hired to do the same work that men do, and are promoted less often.

Married women are also denied a prime method of birth control: the oral contraceptive, known colloquially as the Pill. Though they have a great deal of influence over their husbands when it comes to how many children to have, women are expected to defer to the man, who still bears the responsibility for family planning because it is he who uses condoms, the principal means of birth control in Japan. Japanese health officials have managed to keep the Pill out of Japan for birth control (it may be prescribed by a doctor to treat certain disorders) by arguing that it is not totally safe, that it would encourage promiscuity, that it would discourage condom use as a preventive against AIDS, or that it would drive Japan's already low birth rate even lower. Women argue that oral contraceptives are forbidden because they put too much control over sex in the hands of women.

Traditionally, Japanese men have been uncomfortable with giving women such control because it is regarded as a reversal of sex roles. It is not that men are prudish. Sex has always played a large role in Japanese culture, and the Japanese have long viewed sex as a normal function of the body, like eating and sleeping, not as something sinful or immoral as in Christian countries. But the man is supposed to take the lead in sexual behavior. Married Japanese men who are well off quite often have mistresses who are a separate and important part of the men's lives; the mistresses fulfill a different role from that of the wife, who is expected to bear and raise the children and suffer in silence over her husband's infidelity. On the other hand, if a woman strays from her husband and takes on a lover, she may be outcast, or at least treated harshly. Erotic art, in the form of woodcuts that depict all manner of sexual activity — some of it placing women in a subservient light — has been part of the country's culture for centuries. At one time, prostitution was legal. It was banned after World War II, but it thrives even today as part of Japan's underground "sex industry," a business that caters to men's tastes and whims, often, again, in ways that are humiliating to women. (Contrary to popular Western belief, Japan's geishas, young women trained to entertain and provide lighthearted company for men or groups of men, are not prostitutes, although some do become the mistresses of wealthy men.)

Sadly, many young teenage girls — primarily school dropouts and runaways, some of whom are junior high school age — are forced by gangsters to turn to prostitution, just as in the U.S. Not all of them are Japanese. Filipino and Korean women are often lured to sleezy neighborhoods where they work in massage parlors, bars, dating clubs, and *poruno,* or porn, bookstores and movie houses.

The bookstores generally feature a unique form of erotica known as *manga,* or comic books. Many of these are quite innocent and childish, but others are violent and pornographic, illustrating all kinds of torture and abuse of women. One might argue that it is easy for a Westerner, with a different sense of morality in such matters than the Japanese, to criticize *manga.* Some people say they are harmless and may even serve as a safe outlet for the male readers' sexual tensions. But some *manga* themes — men exerting power over women by humiliating and degrading them, and rough sex just for fun — are certainly not the way to teach respect for one another. While the more violent *manga* are tolerated, many Japanese men and women see them as sick trash, and women's groups, especially, have spoken out against them.

Interestingly, while Japan's "sex industry" is a busy one, and though many Japanese take a more casual view of sex, including homosexual behavior, than mainstream America does, government censors generally crack down on explicit sex. It is another of Japan's mysterious contrasts. Before World War II, kissing in public was forbidden (perhaps because it ruined the stereotype of women as innocents), and it wasn't until 1948 that the first kiss, *kisu* in Japanese, appeared in a movie. Today, movies and magazines that the government deems sexually graphic are carefully scrutinized and "cleaned up." For instance, photographs of nude women in foreign magazines are painted over to erase any trace of pubic hair. This particular taboo also once prevented some drawings by Picasso from being exhibited in a department store art display. And at the movies, the audience can expect to see a large, bright spot of white light covering the actors' exposed bodies during sex scenes. Depending on one's point of view, such censorship is either hypocritical (given the ancient erotic artwork that leaves nothing to the imagination) or an attempt at a moral statement that emulates some of the West's sterner views of sex as it tries to downplay any notions that we may have about Japan's permissiveness.

To be fair, even though Japan generally seems to be quite tolerant about sex, it would be wrong to suggest that the Japanese take it lightly, or that they have no values. While their culture has no religious or moral barrier to sexual relations nor to abortion, the element of shame is always at work, and no Japanese wants to bring shame on himself, especially on herself, or the family. "Better to die with honor than live with shame," says another popular proverb. But for a Japanese, feeling shame is not the same as feeling guilty, as Westerners are apt to do. To the Japanese shame equals disgrace and the "loss of face." When it comes to sex — more so when a woman initiates it — if it will bring shame on someone or the family, it is kept a private matter, not something to be shared with the neighborhood or on television talk shows. Thus, Japanese attitudes toward sex are both permissive and old-fashioned.

Abortion presents Japanese women with a dilemma, even though it is so common that two out of three women have had one. Women everywhere who have abortions are not always comfortable with the difficult choice they have to make. Japanese women are no different, and indeed, given the way their image has been carefully crafted over the centuries, an abortion often causes shame. At a famous Buddhist temple in the middle of Tokyo, one can see ample evidence of this. There, rows and rows of little stone statues of the Buddhist god Jizo fill the garden. Jizo is the patron saint and guardian of the souls of dead children who, according to Buddhist teaching, go to a river in the underworld where a she-devil (that the demon is a woman should raise some questions) makes them pile up stones on the riverbanks. The she-devil promises that if the children build the stones into high towers, they'll be able to climb up into paradise. The children dutifully pile the stones, but other demons scatter them — until Jizo arrives to drive them off and hide the children in the sleeves of his huge coat. Women who have had

Jizo statues

abortions (as well as those who have had miscarriages or children who have died) erect the Jizo statues and place bibs and bonnets on them. They do this in memory of their unborn children and to make peace with their souls. They also place small stones in Jizo's lap to help the children build their towers, and they put clothes on the statue to keep the unborn child warm while he or she works. Sometimes small wooden signs are placed near the statues with inscriptions such as "My baby, I am so sorry. Maybe you will come back to my body in a few years."

With regard to divorce, while it is accepted by a large segment of the population nowadays, many people still view it as a major break in the "rules." One recent book on a woman's divorce failed miserably because many bookstores refused to stock it. "The situation is different in Tokyo," the author said, "but in the countryside everyone would know who bought the book and then neighbors would start to talk about how this or that couple must be thinking about getting divorced."[6]

It is also still very hard for a divorced woman to earn a good living. When there are children, in most cases the wife is given parental authority, but only a few receive child-care support, and those who do don't get very much.

One bright spot in all of this is that most Japanese women are resilient and resourceful, even though that may not always seem evident to the casual observer. During World War II, they took responsibility for their children and elders under horrendous circumstances; today, they are in the forefront of the peace movements, and they run the PTAs and organize the consumer protests. Still, surveys keep cropping up to show that men keep women waiting more often and longer than women do when meeting for a date, that many husbands pay little attention to their wives, and that a lot of Japanese men are fearful and suspicious of strong women.

Edwin Reischauer, former U.S. ambassador to Japan, was once asked about the low esteem men have of women in Japan. His reply is well worth mentioning. "Japanese women have always been felt to be the stronger of the two sexes," the ambassador said, *having a lot more guts than the men do. The men have their own particular Japanese type of macho that they flaunt, but still the Japanese women are the ones who have the real inner strength. If they make that inner strength partly a political strength, why, you may have a very interesting change in Japanese politics. You find that suddenly it becomes important whether or not a man, a politician, is having a mistress, or how he is treating his mistress. Men are being asked to live up to standards they were never asked to live up to before and they suddenly realize they aren't going to be elected if they don't live up to those standards.*[7]

Granted, such a realization is not as common as in the U.S. and other Western nations, and it remains to be seen whether it will become so over the years. Culturally dictated behavior is very difficult to change, and as long as some of the more repressive aspects of tradition are not challenged, the old samurai mentality will hang on. What probably will happen, as it does so often in Japan, is that the role and treatment of women will be a blend of the old and the new, a delicate balancing act between Madame Butterfly and the feminists.

7

The Youth of Japan

Whatis it like to grow up in Japan? Is it different from how most kids in the U.S. grow up? Do Japanese teenagers quarrel with their parents? Do they study more than you do, and do better in school than you? Are they disciplined more often? Do they do drugs, have sex, commit crimes, and want material things? Do they assert themselves? Are they satisfied with their lives?

If you have been fortunate enough to have visited Japan through a student exchange program, you probably lived with a Japanese family. This experience may have given you answers to the above questions. But even then, your answers might not apply to all of Japan's young people. Even though the Japanese are a more homogeneous people than Americans and sometimes behave differently from us as a group because of their culture and traditions, they are not, just as Americans are not, all exactly alike in how they are treated and how they behave as individuals. One sixteen-year-old American exchange student put it as well as anyone:

74

I came to Japan with a lot of mistaken opinions I'd picked up here and there. Now, while I certainly don't know all there is to know about Japan, I at least have direct personal experiences. I think this is vital, that people come to understand one another better. So many times I'd heard: "The Japanese are all quiet and reserved." But that's far from true. Like in America, or any other country I suppose, some people are quiet and some are loud; some are reserved; some are outgoing. Stereotyping countries and peoples can lead to a lot of misunderstanding, and I'm very happy to have had the chance to learn for myself that stereotypes are generally far from true.

Another exchange student, a fifteen-year-old girl, put it this way:

I met kids who were wild, and they did stuff like sniffing glue and skipping school. Some of the guys were real bullies. They looked like they weren't really sure how to treat us American girls, but they were kind of nasty to Japanese girls. And I met kids who were just great. They studied hard, were incredibly respectful, and were even, like, old-fashioned.

We could listen to the remarks of many more American kids who have visited Japan, and they would probably all give us the same mixed picture.

Bearing in mind that we cannot — and should not — stereotype Japanese youths, we can talk generally about what they are like, about how they sometimes differ from Americans your age, and about the things they have in common with you.

First we should note that in Japan, *youth* refers to a definite period of one's life, a distinct stage. Our own dictionary definitions of youth are fairly vague, such as "the time of life when one is young" or "the period between childhood and maturity." But in Japan, *youth* is generally defined as the period from age fourteen to twenty-four. (There is also a word, *seinen,* which means "green years" and is generally applied to youths, young men and young women alike.)

One of the things we hear often about Japan's young people is that they have become more like Americans. Here's what one Japanese sourcebook says about that:

> *Japanese youth have become thoroughly Westernized in their appearance and recreational interests. Avidly copied Western fashions are often mixed with the uniforms many students and company workers wear. They tend to read few books; instead, thick volumes of comics are big sellers. Attitudes toward sex appear to be very relaxed. Watching television is probably the most popular leisure activity, followed by comic books, sports, and going to discotheques. College students spend a fair amount of time chatting or reading in coffeehouses.*[1]

It is true that Western influence (*Western* usually means American when it's used in Japan) is strong in Japan. Japanese students routinely study English. American movie stars and rock musicians are household names. Jeans and running shoes and sweats are standard leisure wear. English expressions, or words derived from English words — like *mai kaa,* for "my car," and *mai pesu,* for "my pace" — are cool. The *mai* generation shows other signs of Westernization: French perfume and French wine are in, as are American cigarettes, L. L. Bean moccasins, Wendy's, McDonald's (it's called Makudonarudo over there), Dunkin'

Donuts, Tokyo Disneyland, and giant billboard pictures of Clint Eastwood and James Dean.

Many Japanese teens also talk more these days about becoming "independent individuals" like their American counterparts, and to prove that they are serious, some of them criticize their parents, skip school, reject the way of life that has been mapped out for them, and spend most of their time in video game arcades. At the end of any given day, they might get rid of their school uniforms — stiff black military-cut clothes for the boys and long black skirts for the girls — dress up in outlandish Western clothes, and sneak out to a park to listen to loud music and dance. Every Sunday afternoon, in fact, hundreds of teens dress up in fifties or punk clothing, or as gangsters out of American movies, and head for Yoyogi Park in Tokyo to hang out. Some join motorcycle gangs, wear leather jackets, and ride motorbikes without mufflers through towns in the early morning hours. A few turn violent, beating up their teachers and classmates, and sometimes even committing murder. Others, alienated from their families or unable to bear the pressures of school or work, kill themselves — Japan has one of the world's highest teenage suicide rates. As we have said, the Japanese are a people caught between the old and the new, and the young, especially, feel the weight of their society's stern demands, something that American teens do not usually have to deal with.

But for all of their seeming adoption of many Western ways, have Japanese youths really become thoroughly Westernized? Many observers, including this writer, believe they have not. *Westernized* means a lot more than wearing Western-style clothes or listening to Western rock music. Japanese teenagers are still Japanese, and given the rigid cultural framework they live in — a framework that shows no signs of collapsing — it is doubtful they'll ever lose their essential Japanese values and perspective. Japanese kids may want a little more fun than their parents did, but most of them are still strongly conformist and cling to traditions such as respect for the elderly, dedication to the group, bowing when they greet one another, and following the desires of their parents that they get through school, compete for places in the best universities and jobs in the most prestigious companies, and search for the best possible marriage mate.

The problem is that every time a Japanese does something out of the ordinary — dyeing his or her hair purple, arguing with a parent or teacher, or just hanging out somewhere — a politician, a newspaper or a television station makes a big thing out of it, and it is held up as one more example of the awful influence of the West or of a major change taking place in Japanese kids. The argument that the current generation of young people is worse than the ones before is not new, however, and is offered by adults in most other countries, including the United States. In Japan, where the emphasis is on achieving and on holding fast to the old order, it is understandable why any deviation from the norm is considered a tragedy.

Ian Buruma, a writer on popular Japanese culture, refers to Japanese teenage rebels as the country's "outrageous conformists," and he points out that even their strange clothes and bizarre behavior are rooted in stern tradition. Singling out Japan's version of our youth gangs, the *zoku,* or tribe, as an example, Buruma writes that Japan itself is divided into many small tribes, from trading companies with their own songs, uniforms, and philosophies, to youth groups sharing a common style. One of these *zoku* is called the Amegurazoku, which takes its name from the movie *American Graffiti*. The tribe's style is a takeoff on what Japanese kids think American youth was like in the fifties. Here's what Buruma has to say about this group:

> *They wear wraparound shades, slicked-back ducktail and sugar-puff bouffant hairdos, tight leather pants, Cuban heels, fake leopard-skin jackets, at-the-hop petticoats, and ribbons. They even pull the same surly faces as their idols, mouths fixed in Presley sneers. All this was bound to set the tired old tongues clucking once again about "Americanization" and "rebellious youth." And cluck they did.*
>
> *Yet it is all an elaborate fake, a beautifully studied act that only looks like the real thing. Everything down to the minutest gesture is practiced over and over again, just as a sushi chef might spend two years learning the only correct way to cut a piece of tuna. One can observe boys combing each other's duck-tails so they are just right and senior girls teaching newcomers the only correct way to dance to a certain number. They even stage fights in pure Blackboard Jungle style — but without touching each other. In brief, rock 'n roll is learnt as if it were any other Japanese art.[2]*

Unlike American gangs, the *zoku* don't get into fights with each other. On the contrary, because rigid formality can be used by the Japanese to express their separateness, when different *zoku* meet on the same turf they go through complicated courtesy rituals. Even the motorcycle gangs, says Buruma, are generally a relatively harmless lot, in no way comparable to our Hell's Angels:

> *The Bosozoku ("Speeding Tribe") seek their thrills by riding around in packs of bikes and even cars (often purchased by indulgent parents) — breaking the speed limit, honking horns, and giving the police a hard time. The violence that does occur is usually among themselves — when a member breaks the group code, for instance.*[3]

Japanese kids do their own thing — but only according to certain rules and to a timetable. Most kids, for example, would never dream of behaving outrageously while shopping in a department store or while visiting a park on an ordinary day. But if there is a place and a time for uncharacteristic behavior, they'll take advantage of it and show another side of their personality. I recall going to a football game in Tokyo in which two visiting U.S. teams played an exhibition game. As teenagers streamed into the stadium, ushers handed out team pennants at random. Teens with one team's pennant were assigned seats on one side of the field; those with the other team's sat opposite. Though the kids weren't fans of either team, during play they dutifully cheered and waved their pennants whenever "their team" made gains or scored — all of the cheering and clapping on signal from the professional cheerleaders for each side. Since the Japanese aren't among the world's biggest football fans, the fact that they could act like those of you who appreciate the game says something about their ability to emulate Western behavior.

This does not mean, of course, that Japanese kids don't really like American sports or clothes or behavior, or that when they imitate, say, an American rocker, they don't have a real appreciation of his or her music. Most Japanese kids truly like American style and trends, and insofar as Western music is concerned, whether it be rock or rap or classical, they often have a real ear for it, and a number of musicians perform it professionally, and quite well at that.

Japanese youths are, after all, more plugged into the world at large than their parents and grandparents were, and they have more money to spend on fun things. They travel and mingle with foreigners far more easily; the vast majority who attend U.S. schools are quite happy here and generally get along very well with their American classmates. Their attitude toward sex is far more liberal than their parents'. And, aware that their country is no longer a second-stringer, they seem to lack the feeling of inferiority that plagued their grandparents who, humiliated, had to make a go of life after their country was defeated in World War II.

But for all the differences between today's Japanese youth and the previous generation, we cannot, again, forget that along with modernization, Japanese values still play a key role in the lives of the country's young people.

At the core of those values is the educational system. Structured and strict, it shapes the daily life of every Japanese young person from kindergarten through high school. On the surface, the school system looks much like ours, with its levels from grade school to four-year colleges, and a collection of kindergartens, technical schools, and schools for the disabled. But the way the Japanese study, and the amount of time they put into it, differ greatly from our own system.

In general, all the schools, with the glaring exception of the colleges, have a reputation for being stiff and stern. Uniforms are often required, and sometimes shaved heads for the boys; there is no smoking, no true expression of one's views, no deviation from the lesson plan, which emphasizes learning by memorization and by mechanical repetition of information. Some schools tell the students what movies they can and cannot see, what coffee shops to frequent or avoid. Sometimes, students are abused physically — in one notable case, a junior high school teacher was accused of punching his pupils and pouring water over their heads because they failed to report a smoking incident. Another time, a principal locked two teenage students for nearly two days in a metal shed in 100-degree temperatures for breaking school rules; both died.

Such incidents do not, of course, occur frequently. But students who disobey rules can expect discipline. Education, in the words of one official of the Japan Teachers Union, is conducted in an atmosphere of "commands, orders, regulations, and penalties." Adds a member of the Board of Education in Tokyo, "In Japanese schools, teachers do the talking and students do the listening. They only respond when asked a question. Therefore, Japanese have trouble expressing themselves."[4] When they do express themselves — as Japanese students who have studied in the U.S. sometimes do when they return to school in Japan — they are usually soon put in their place by a surprised teacher.

The goal of all this rigidity is to acquire knowledge, something that sits quite well with Japan's industries, which recruit the best students from the best schools. In U.S. schools, although the accumulation of factual knowledge is important, the goal is to teach students to think for themselves and to solve problems.

What do Japanese students learn? Just about everything you do, and sometimes they learn things a grade or two before you do. They start learning English in the seventh grade, learn to read music and play an instrument in grade school, and study Chinese and Japanese classical literature in high school, along with subjects many American students usually don't get into until college — inorganic chemistry, mechanical physics, advanced physics, statistics, and calculus. They don't have as many electives as American students do, sticking instead with the basics — math, social studies, science, English — several times a week all through junior high and high school. Moreover, they go to school more days than most American kids — 240 days a year, half-time on Saturdays; in the U.S. most public school students go to classes for between 180 and 200 days. Although classroom hours are similar to those of U.S. schools, Japanese kids spend almost three times as much time every week as you do on schoolwork; before they graduate from elementary school, they're doing five to six hours of homework a night, more than most of you are assigned.

Almost all students go on to high school, and the country is almost 100 percent literate. Exceptionally bright kids do not skip grades, and kids who do poorly do not get special attention and are not kept back. Everyone is automatically promoted to the next grade, no matter how much or how little he or she knows. This is because Japanese students are not supposed to stand out — whether as overachievers or underachievers. To do so would tag them as "different," and not only educators but parents feel that is shameful. In U.S. schools, such "different" students receive special treatment. In Japan what is important is the group, not an individual student's progress, and it is the whole class that must move ahead. If a student starts to shine, he or she simply keeps pace with the rest of the class, no matter how boring that may be; a poor student tries to keep up, comfortable in knowing that he or she won't be kept back because that would be too embarrassing for student and parents.

Even though the group is the focus, Japan does reward the brightest students. Since most of the top executives and government officials graduated from the country's best universities, the competition to get into those universities is fierce. Most American students take exams only to get promoted and to graduate, but Japanese kids take tests all along the line to get

Preschoolers in a juku

into schools. The process often starts with preschoolers, two and three years old, who sometimes have to take tests to get into a nursery school. Wearing headbands with slogans such as "Certain victory in examination," preschoolers sweat through a supplementary school called a *juku,* or cram school, to prepare them for the tests they'll have to take to get into prestigious grade schools later on. Grade-school students have to take competitive exams to get into prestigious junior high and high schools, and if they need to, attend a *juku* after hours and on their days off. Here's how one young cram school student described the experience:

> *I study five days a week at a* juku. *The class begins at 5 P.M. After school, I return home to fetch textbooks and a packed dinner, and then go to* juku. *The classes finish at 9 P.M. If necessary, I can get private guidance until 11 P.M. It takes me about thirty minutes to go home, and I arrive at about midnight. I do my homework, play games on a computer and go to bed around 2 A.M.*[5]

Working hand in hand with the authoritarian education system to keep the pressure on are the kids' mothers. The Japanese have a special name for some of them: *kyoiku-mama,* or "education-obsessed mom." It's up to her to see that her son or daughter tries to be number one, and that he or she gets into a good school. Mothers in Japan are often quite indulgent, allowing their kids a good deal of freedom, and even enduring abuse from them, as long as their children bring home the grades. Needless to say, many moms spend more time helping or forcing their children to study than playing with them, and with more and more women working in Japan, and with fathers coming home late every night, there is often little time for family recreation.

High school seniors probably have it the worst because there aren't many student slots open in the best universities. About a third make it through "Examination Hell," as it's called, and get in on the first try; others have to do more work in a *juku* and try again. Interestingly, while it is most difficult to get into a prestigious college, once the fortunate students do, life is a lot easier for them — in fact college has been called a fun vacation because a lot of students feel it's their reward for going through cram schools and the endless Examination Hells. Academic demands are generally light, cutting classes is standard behavior, professors frequently show up late for class and leave early, and there is a lot of socializing and sports. The main reason a lot of Japanese students are in the best universities is to get a top job — all that's required is that he (and it's usually a he) be there. The companies have been waiting for the graduates, and recruit them while they're in school.

Do all of the tests, the cramming, and the discipline mean that Japanese students are better and smarter than other kids? A few years ago, scientists reported that Japanese students did better in math than Americans, and scored eleven points higher in IQ tests. Some people suggested that the brains of Japanese kids were somehow "wired" differently and that genetic factors made them smarter. It's doubtful that is the case. Even Japanese educators agree that the enviable record of Japanese students is due to their experience with Examination Hells, which have made them efficient test takers but not necessarily smarter. "It is indeed the environment rather than heredity that enables Japanese to perform so well in testing," said one U.S. university professor. "Americans, if they are beginning to feel inadequate, should be concerned not about their mental endowment but about their education system."[6]

Most Japanese youths who get through the tortuous education process turn out fine, and the ones who go on to good jobs usually stick with them. But, understandably, the high level of stress kids endure over the years sometimes breaks them down, physically and emotionally. To cope with the stress, many kids guzzle energy drinks sold for hard-working adults, which contain caffeine and vitamins. A lot of Japanese students have ulcers, constipation, and chronic fatigue, and some, even as young as ten, take their own lives.

Still, for all of its failings, the rigid system works well for most Japanese graduates. The people it churns out are just what the nation's high-powered industries want: hard-working company men and women who don't talk much about individuality. They have sopped up knowledge like sponges, and that's what the tough school years are all about.

The ones who haven't cracked the books and the ones who've tried but still haven't gotten into the schools their parents wanted for them face a different story. They soon find life to be an endless round of ordinary jobs with few benefits. In addition, they feel unusual. A psychologist at a women's college explained it this way:

This sense is deeply associated with feelings of worthlessness, shamefulness, and alienation. All of it seems to be greatly influenced by the stereotyped sense of values in contemporary society in which a good school record and an academic career as well as sociability and cheerfulness are thought to be important.[7]

Many poor students resent the ones who get high marks; although they aren't kept back, they're quite often ignored by their teachers. They know that they don't fit in, and because little is done to improve their performance they often just give up. Other times they rebel against the harsh rules. They might turn on their teachers, beat up students who seem to be spending too much time on homework or in cram schools, miss classes, or refuse to go to school at all. An increasing number use drugs like methamphetamine — "speed" or "ice" as it's known on the street — and get arrested.

One girl in her first year at a strict junior high school with regulations that included the type of underwear she had to wear and participation in a variety of extracurricular clubs, had this to say:

> *I liked basketball, I just didn't like the club. When you met a* senpai *[senior club member] on the street, you had to bow three times. Returning home after practice, you weren't allowed to get home before your* senpai. *Even though I lived close to school, I didn't get home until eight every night because I had to walk the* senpai *home.*

The girl eventually started leaving school early, riding her bike far away and then coming home late at night. Then she started pretending to go to school at six in the morning, coming home after her mother had left for work. Other times, she would just hide in her closet with the futons, sweating, but it was better, she said, than going to school.[8]

Kids who have to live overseas because their fathers must work outside Japan for a few years often have their own special problems when they go home. Most Japanese children who accompany their parents to another country benefit from their stay; they usually hone their English or some other language to a conversational level, and they learn a lot about their host country's culture. Back in Japan, however, they are referred to as "the returnees," and sometimes they have a difficult time readjusting to their smaller homes or apartments, spending more time at home — overseas their parents usually entertained more than in Japan and went out more often — and getting back into the routine of cramming and exams for school admission. They often have trouble keeping up with classes and making friends, and even have problems with the Japanese language. If the returnees are too fluent in English, some teachers conclude that their minds are now programmed in the English language, a sign that the kids have forgotten how to be Japanese. Some of the returnees even have to be trained all over again to use chopsticks, an embarrassing exercise since the Japanese have been using them for more than a thousand years. (But then, kids who never went overseas also have trouble with the slender eating utensils: a 1990 study on children's ability to hold chopsticks found that only 10.6 percent of the primary school students were able to use them correctly. Adults, too, seem to be having a problem with chopsticks: another study found that only 60 percent of people between the ages of thirty and forty could handle them well.[9]) A Japanese psychiatric social worker, Tazuko Shibusawa, once referred to the difficulty a returnee has in re-adapting to Japanese culture as the "toothpaste" effect. By that she meant that toothpaste is easy to get out of the tube, but impossible to get back in.[10]

School districts don't always agree on how the returnees should be retrained. Some give them special training or allow them to enroll in lower-level classes; other districts refuse to do so, and just throw the returnees into the mill. A few of the kids are resented, even bullied, by youths who never went overseas, and sometimes overly demanding teachers treat them more harshly than they do the others. "It was like I had been on vacation for the three years I spent in the States," said one junior high student who was preparing for high school entrance exams, "and now I had to pay for it."

We mentioned that some Japanese kids are alienated and turn violent. This happens in America, too, as we all know. In Japan, such behavior is nothing new. During the 1960s and 1970s, many Japanese students protested, sometimes violently, against the Vietnam War and political corruption. A lot of universities were shut down during those turbulent years. Even before that, in the aftermath of World War II, youth crime and protest were widespread. With so many vagrant war orphans in the devastated cities, it was no surprise that thievery and robbery by young people was common, along with the abuse of stimulant drugs; many young people also rebelled against what they saw as social injustices and a lack of emphasis on the rights of individuals, and created major disturbances.

In recent years, a minority of Japanese youths has given parents and educators some cause for concern, although nothing like what happened after World War II and during the Vietnam War period. The behavior of these misfits goes far beyond wearing wild clothing and doing all those other fearsome "Western" things. Some of these rebellious teens seem to care little for their studies, and refuse to attend classes. They are called *tokokyohi,* which means "wandering bats," or "school refusals." On the other hand, some study so much that they become listless, and refuse even to play, even when they have the time. The Japanese call these kids "bean sprouts" because they grow up quickly but have no substance. Other kids physically assault their teachers, weaker children, or even their parents; some steal bikes, bust up school furniture, deface property, shoplift, and, as one report on youth from the prime minister's office put it, "perform acts that harm one's own or other people's moral character, such as drinking, smoking and brawling."[11]

It is hard to say just how widespread or how serious such behavior is. Depending on the source, it is either quite alarming or vastly overblown. What seems to be clear, however, is that while statistics for "juvenile delinquency" and dropping out of school are not as high as in other countries, they are increasing. Aware of the potential danger, everyone from the police to the Education Ministry issues regular appeals for more moral guidance, establishment of crime-prevention councils, and community activities "to protect youth from delinquency."

The youth issue that seems to have received the most attention in Japan as well as abroad is what the Japanese press calls *ijime,* or "bullying." This refers to students who beat up their teachers and classmates, something that we all know too well happens in America. In fact, with something like 100,000 teachers assaulted here by students in any given year, along with countless students stabbed or shot by their classmates in some inner-city schools, school violence has become almost commonplace. But in Japan, where crime is not as widespread as in the U.S., and where courtesy and respect for authority, especially teachers, are seemingly programmed into Japanese genes, such behavior is akin to anarchy.

The police regularly handle hundreds of school violence cases every year, and several thousand students have been placed "under guidance." Among the more brutal attacks: a group of junior high students forced a schoolmate to eat grass, then poured acid down his back; two boys, a fifth grader and a third grader, slashed three schoolgirls with paper cutters, then ripped up their own uniforms, school caps, and knapsacks; a fifteen-year-old junior high student blew up his teacher's car with dynamite because he didn't like the teacher's demands; another teen beat up his teacher with a metal baseball bat after he told another student not to spit on the floor; a vicious female gang at an all-girl private school regularly dragged achieving students by their hair into restrooms, kicked them, flogged them with belts, burned their chests with cigarettes, forced objects into their genitals, and shaved off their body hair; a gang of teens, armed with bats, knives, and smoke-bombs, disrupted a graduation ceremony; a fifteen-year-old threw a Molotov cocktail through the window of a high school because his teacher had cut the student's long hair. In some of the cases, bullied students, like the youth who was made to eat grass, have killed themselves.

Nor is the violence confined to the schools. From time to time, the media highlights cases such as the son who beat his mother to death because she was constantly at him to pass the strenuous university entrance exams, or so-called "hobo hunting," in which gangs of youths beat up vagrants. In one such attack, teenage boys killed three vagrants and seriously injured a dozen more; they told police they had gone on the rampage "just for fun."

Incidents like these occasionally occur in the U.S., too, but it has been pointed out that America's teenage and school violence is often the result of racial conflict, drugs, or some other social ill. In Japan, which has none of our racial problems and where drug abuse is not as prevalent as in the U.S., the school violence often seems to be a personal attack in response to pressures at home or in school.

The current wave of school violence in Japan is often seen as a sign of the rapidly shifting values and needs of many young people, most of whom have been raised in relative affluence and influenced by a media and an entertainment industry that often takes its cues from the West in emphasizing individuality, sex, and not uncommonly, violence. There are other pat scapegoats: permissive parents, the demise of tightly knit neighborhoods where everyone knew everyone else, and their replacement by apartment-stacks that make strangers of the residents; a decline in parental authority, notably that of the father, who was once as fearsome to Japanese kids as thunder, earthquakes, and fire.

Then there is the standard conservative line that the violence can be traced back to the American occupation, which chipped away at Japan's traditions — those that emphasized national-ism, morality, group loyalty, and the obligations of sons and daughters toward their parents — and replaced it with a system that focused on the self and liberal thinking. Some years ago, Soichi Morita, a judge in the Tokyo Family Court, said some-thing that many Japanese still accept:

> *What has happened is that the order on which society rested and which, for better or for worse, gave life its traditions has been largely destroyed, without any clear-cut new image of the family emerging to take its place.*[12]

Predictably, modernization (sometimes just another word for Westernization or American), along with the liberal changes brought about by the occupation, are also often blamed for the perceived rise in promiscuous behavior among Japanese teens.

Other critics put the blame on parents who spend more time training their kids to pass examinations than on sex education.

While only a relative few Japanese teens are very sexually active, the number of kids who are having sex is increasing, and young Japanese girls are more sexually experienced than boys. Most Japanese teens believe that having sex outside marriage is okay as long as the partners love each other. Condoms are a popular method of birth control because the Pill, which is the most effective means of artificial birth control, is still outlawed in Japan as medically unsafe for general use.

Sometimes, sex results in unwanted pregnancies, as in the U.S. and elsewhere, and abortion as a form of birth control is a common way out. Among teens the abortion rate is believed to be around one out of one hundred. More than 30,000 abortions are obtained by teenagers in a year, many of them more than three months into the pregnancy, a period when most abortions are to be avoided because of the high risk to the mother. The current abortion law, enacted after World War II partly to get rid of children fathered by occupying soldiers, is quite liberal, allowing young women to claim that having a child would endanger their health "for economic reasons" — the grounds used by the vast majority of Japanese women who seek abortions. One often hears a Japanese say that getting an abortion in their country is about as common as taking aspirin or having a tooth extracted, and some doctors routinely ask a pregnant woman if she really wants to have the child.

What about drug use among Japan's teenagers? Marijuana, "speed," paint thinner, and cocaine are the most abused substances. But while the number of Japanese teens who use drugs seems to be increasing, their number is nothing compared to the situation in the United States. Consider these U.S. statistics:

a third of all U.S. students have tried marijuana before leaving the ninth grade; nearly two-thirds will have done so before they're out of high school; one of six high school seniors will have been a daily user at some time in their lives; nearly 20 percent of high school seniors have tried cocaine.[13] Add to that the nearly five million American teens who have a drinking problem and the some 800,000 Americans, many of them teenagers, who are addicted to heroin, and the U.S. picture is a grim one indeed. With only 5 percent of the world's population, we consume half of the world's drugs.

Japanese kids, like Americans, experiment with drugs. "Young people tend to take narcotic drugs as well as stimulants out of mere curiosity," an official of the National Police Agency's drug enforcement division observed recently. "It appears that, from the standpoint of those young people, a soothing sense of belonging to a group can be generated by taking illicit drugs."[14] Whether the drug situation in Japan will ever match that of the U.S. and other countries remains to be seen. Before 1945, there was little illicit drug use in Japan, but after World War II there were serious problems. Government crackdowns seemed to control the abuse for a time.

At present, abuse of stimulants such as methamphetamine is on the rise among the young, and drug enforcement officials consider them and marijuana to be the major sources of concern. Alcohol abuse is also increasing. Indeed the Japanese now drink far more than they have ever done; liquor is readily available from coin-operated vending machines that are just about everywhere, and much of the advertising for alcoholic beverages is aimed at young people.

Japan has become an affluent society, and its young people, though they still generally toe the traditional line, have been affected by that affluence. Many are demanding more time to do what they want to do, and that includes drinking and drugs; they are trying hard to be modern, looking for kicks, visiting the United States — more than 30,000 Japanese youths are now living and studying here — and even expressing dissatisfaction with what is expected of them in school and at work.

The causes of drug and alcohol abuse are many and complex. If such abuse truly becomes a social trend in Japan, the country will inevitably see the emergence of yet another drug culture with all the problems that go with it. While Japan's increasing affluence has changed the country's teens, the reverse of that trend will also have an adverse effect. The Japanese economy at this writing is faltering, and bankruptcies, robbery, murder, suicides, and mental depression are becoming more commonplace. Just as good times breed loosened behavior that may include recreational drug abuse, bad times trigger escapist drug abuse — the use of drugs to forget one's problems — and other troubling behavior. In 1991, some 16,000 people were arrested for drug law violations in Japan, nine hundred of them youths, under age twenty, arrested for methamphetamine abuse.[15] The numbers are not large given the population of the country. But arrests are only a small part of the picture. The number of people abusing drugs is probably far more than just the number of those who have been arrested.

All we can hope for the future is that whatever it is that makes the Japanese so Japanese will prevail, that they will continue to draw on their own unique strengths and ability to cope and adapt, that their ingrained sense of "face" will never disappear. We can also hope that Japan's teens will not try to emulate the worst of all that they see and hear and admire about the West.

How does one sum up the youth of Japan? It's not easy to do so. But everyone seems to have an answer. They have been called industrious, lazy; obedient, rebellious; group-oriented, selfish; modern, traditional; respectful, and neglectful. Here is how one government agency has assessed Japan's kids:

A survey on how youth lives shows that they attach importance to their own lives. In other words, they tend to find satisfaction in life from friends around them or from their personal deeds. Young people are increasingly satisfied with their present status. This reflects the rise in family income, the improvement of the living standard and the increase of leisure time. On the whole, they take a positive view of the society in which they live and therefore have a tendency to maintain their present lives.

They generally prefer the easy way to the hard way in getting things done. In other words, they are less enthusiastic about slow and steady ways than about easy and eye-catching ways. They lack patience and perseverance and try to realize their wishes without effort. At the same time, they are serious about doing things in which they have a keen interest.

In human relations, young people are oriented toward friendship, and they emphasize their personal lives. Thus, more and more young people attach importance to human relations. Present-day youth seeks feelings of harmony in all areas of their social activity. They are emotionally oriented to harmony, setting great store by the atmosphere of friendly encounters.

Their impressions of being "selfish," "socially indifferent," and "irresponsible" are evaluated negatively. On the other hand, the impressions of being "individualistic" and "ambitious" are highly rated. The survey also indicates that young people have a more negative image of themselves than adults have of them.[16]

How much of that can actually be applied across the board is debatable. Surveys that draw general conclusions are important, but their focus on "they," "them," and "their" often neglect the individual "he" and "she" who make up the group being studied. If you really want to know what Japanese kids are like, you'll have to meet more of them. There's nothing better than personal contact for getting rid of stereotypes, by seeing first-hand the differences and similarities among people.

8

The Industrious Japanese

The cram schools and other hallmarks of the highly structured Japanese educational system may put stress on a lot of teenagers, but that is the price they pay for the reward many of them receive for studying so hard. That reward is more often than not a good job and a fairly secure future, something that fewer and fewer Americans can expect these days.

What kind of work will Japanese kids do when their school ordeal is over? Well, depending on how far they go in school, it isn't much different from what American teenagers will do. The Japanese are engineers and bankers, doctors and scientists and teachers, machine operators and nurses, carpenters and clerks, secretaries and salespeople. Some work on assembly lines, on farms, or in shops, civil service offices, and restaurants.

There is really nothing that we do in the United States that the Japanese do not do. That was not always the case, however. Only thirty years ago, about half the population of Japan worked the land or as fishermen. Today, along with a small percentage of farmers, there are only about 500,000 people working in the fishing industry — but that is adequate to handle the catching and processing of more than ten million tons of fish a year. The vast majority of the Japanese people now work in the various service and manufacturing industries we know so well in our country.

There are, however, some notable differences between the U.S. and Japan when it comes to work. One is the concept of guaranteed lifetime employment for some workers. In Japan, once they are hired, they generally stay with a company until retirement, which is around age fifty-five, and their pay is determined by their length of service. (A number of companies now take one's ability into account, too, however.) Switching jobs, as occurs frequently among American workers, is not as widespread in Japan because it is seen as a sign that the worker hasn't got what it takes to become a success, so workers tend to stick it out. Still, a growing number of young people who feel stifled by Japan's rigid seniority system and want to climb the ladder more quickly are less hesitant these days about moving on to another job, a trend that Japan's old guard finds hard to accept. The Japanese even have a name for young people who move from one job to another in a short space of time — second freshmen. More young people, especially women, are also looking for temporary work so that they can have time either to start their own businesses or return to school.

Contrary to what many Americans believe, not everyone in Japan is granted lifetime employment. It is usually reserved for the most qualified graduates from prestigious universities who must compete for positions in the large companies. Perhaps a third of Japanese workers have such job security; the vast majority of Japanese workers are employed not by the large companies — Americans tend to think all Japanese work for

Toyota, Honda, or Sony — but by medium-size and small firms, which provide few benefits, low salaries, and very little job security.

Large Japanese companies are run like communities or large families. Many provide employees and their families with dormitory housing, recreational facilities, stores, and a hospital. Employees and employers are said to be fiercely competitive; long hours are considered a necessary sign of loyalty and devotion to one's company and are usually requirements for staying ahead. "Men are mortal, but the company goes on forever," said the head of one of Japan's largest firms. This statement reflects the way managers and workers alike generally feel about the company that employs them. Trainees in many of the major companies regularly shout company slogans, sing company songs, wear uniforms, and memorize and recite on demand stern rules of business practice such as "Whatever hardships confront me, I will not surrender my objective, working until late at night to the best of my ability to accomplish my goals with unremitting strength of will." One can hardly imagine a General Motors employee or an American teenager working the counter at McDonald's chanting those words. Sometimes, the sloganeering takes on a warlike tone. In fact, many over-demanding Japanese managers (and not a few American ones) swear by a more than three-hundred-year-old book on samurai sword strategy (samurais were the warrior-aristocrats of ancient Japan) written by Miyamoto Musashi, a "sword-saint" who killed many men in duels and was regarded as unbeatable. Called *A Book of Five Rings* (the rings are the chapters), it draws on Japanese and Chinese philosophy, emphasizes mental discipline, and describes the best way to use the sword and martial arts, and how to attack the enemy effectively. Because Musashi suggested that his hints could be used in any situation calling for plans and tactics, Japanese businessmen have seized on it as the perfect guide to running sales campaigns and other business practices. A sample quotation from the book that a company manager might use to fire up a salesperson: "If you learn and attain this strategy you will never lose, even to 20 or 30 enemies. You must utterly cut the enemy down so that he does not recover his position."

With that kind of pep talk, it is no wonder that few Japanese workers dare to go home earlier than the boss (who knows they fear him and is quite often apt to stay late just to keep his staff working). Indeed, one big difference between the Japanese and American work forces is the working hours. In 1987, the standard workweek in Japan was forty-eight hours; today it is around forty-three, compared to an average of 38.5 in the U.S. Many Japanese workers put in far more hours than the statistics show, however. While people who work for the national government now work five days a week, six-day workweeks are the rule rather than the exception (only 10 percent of the nation's companies have a five-day workweek), and so, too, is after-hours work in the office, or in local bars and restaurants, as young *sararimen* (salarymen) meet with customers and business associates. Auto workers typically work twelve-hour shifts, and some Japanese salespeople put in up to seventy hours a week, with no overtime pay. Indeed, while "workaholism" is showing some signs of easing, it still characterizes most Japanese workers.

"In rating personnel," said one management consultant, "Japanese managers tend to favor people who work long hours — unlike in the West, where the question is how much you have accomplished in a given time period."[1] Typical Japanese workaholics might even give up vacations and holidays, fearing that if they take too much time off, they'll be left out when bonus and promotion time comes around. Sometimes the company emphasizes this idea by posting notices warning that if workers take too many days off, either planned or unexpectedly, they could make things difficult for fellow workers and would, indeed, upset the boss. One company has a slogan that says "Take vacation, but without causing a burden for others." Then there's the Japanese proverb that says "A smiling boy seldom proves a good servant." As one young executive put it, "If I came home at five o'clock every night, my wife would worry that I didn't care about my rivals at the office, and that they'd get a raise before me." Before you judge Japanese companies and their workers too harshly, remember that they are no different from some of ours. Many of our managers make their employees stay around later than they should, take advantage of an employee's guilt over his or her going on two weeks' vacation all at once, and promote people or give them raises only if they've gone far beyond what they're paid to do.

Whether or not Japanese workers actually like working long hours is a question that has been debated for some time. Certainly, company presidents are pleased when the image of the gung-ho Japanese worker is presented abroad, because it sets the Japanese worker apart from just about everyone else. But Japanese labor unions are far weaker than our own, which means that company managers can pretty much set the rules and workers have little recourse but to go along, like it or not. The unions have also traditionally favored job security for their workers, and they are willing to give in on long hours and hard work to maintain that benefit. The fact is, however, that Japanese like to play just as much as we do. With the rise in

Japan's standard of living, an increasing number of Japanese are paying more attention to leisure time, and even object strongly to having to work beyond normal hours. There has been more talk of a standard five-day workweek recently, and more and more workers are taking vacations and spending more time with their families. According to a recent survey by the prime minister's office, the young, especially, regard leisure as more important than any other activity.

A few years ago, an American journalist looking into the Japanese work ethic quoted the director of the Japan Youth Research Institute as saying, "Workers screw in a bolt and when the clock strikes five they stop turning." The writer went on to paint this picture of some other cracks developing in the work pattern in Japan:

> *More surprising is the growing reluctance of college graduates to push themselves as hard as they once did. The change is detectable even at prestigious companies that attract the most ambitious young people. An editor at* Yomiuri Shimbun, *the country's largest daily newspaper, notes that three of the freshman reporters the paper hired [recently] have quit, complaining that the work is too hard. That's extraordinary compared with previous years when it was rare to have anyone drop out after surviving the competition of hundreds of college graduates for those jobs. The same editor says that his own 21-year-old son, a college senior, is looking for a job that isn't too hard and will give him plenty of vacation time. . . .*
>
> *A decade ago, the Japanese language contained no idiom like the West's "Thank God it's Friday." Today many young office workers exchange salutations of "Hana no kinyobi," which freely translated means "Friday's the greatest." They take long-*

ish Friday lunch hours and let their thoughts drift to the weekend social calendar. Sports and friends, not work and study, give meaning to life, young Japanese said in a recent government survey.[2]

This new attitude raises the question whether the Japanese, for all their longer hours on the job, do actually work harder than we do. No one can say that as a people they do or do not. Some Japanese, deeply committed to the idea of the group pulling together as hard as its members are able, drive themselves mercilessly. Others are forced to work almost to the point of exhaustion. Here is how one Japanese journalist who worked for six months some years ago on an automobile manufacturer's assembly line described the cruel, robotlike behavior that was required:

No one can understand how it works without experiencing it. Almost as soon as I begin, I am dripping with sweat. Somehow, I learn the order of the work motions, but I am totally unable to keep up with the speed of the line. My work gloves make it difficult to grab as many tiny bolts as I need, and how many precious moments do I waste doing just that? I do my best but I can barely finish one gear box out of three within the fixed length of time. . . . The line is a machine, and the humans working at it are required to operate with machinelike accuracy. The line demands speed — relentless, mechanical and unchanging. . . . I'm thirsty as hell, but workers can neither smoke nor drink water. Going to the toilet is out of the question . . . during working hours we can't even talk. Who could have invented a system like this? It's designed to make workers do nothing but work and to prevent any kind of rest. . . . The conveyor starts at 6 A.M. and doesn't stop until 11 A.M. One box of transmissions arrives on the conveyor belt every minute and twenty seconds with unerring precision. When the line stops at 11 o'clock, we tear off our gloves and leave our positions as quickly as we can. We wash our greasy hands and run to the toilet, then rush to the canteen about a hundred yards away where we wait in another line to get our food. After standing five hours, my legs are numb and stiff. My new safety shoes are so heavy that I feel I can barely move.[3]

Some workers are driven so hard, mentally as well as physically, that they die from job-related illnesses or accidents. The Japanese call this *karoshi*, which means death by overwork. Some even kill themselves because of the stress of their jobs. The majority of these deaths occur among young salarymen, and so prevalent have such suicides become that a *karoshi* hotline has been established. In one recent case, a young man killed himself at his office when a bell rang to signal the beginning of the workday.

Fortunately not all Japanese workers react to job stress this way, nor do all of them give their all for their companies. As in the United States and just about everywhere on earth, a large number do as little as possible and grumble if they feel put upon. The difference, however, is that the Japanese rarely grumble at authority or in public — they generally complain at home and to their friends — and certainly not often to a foreigner. To do otherwise is considered un-Japanese.

Not long ago, our newspapers and television networks spread remarks of Japan's prime minister that seemed to indicate his belief that Americans lacked a "work ethic." Another Japanese politician allegedly said that Americans were lazy and that a third of our work force was illiterate; still another said that we turned out inferior products. Many Americans felt insulted, and one television advertisement for an American product in competition with a Japanese one prefaced the sales pitch with an announcer saying in an offended voice, "Well, excuse us!" Whether the remarks by the Japanese were accurate, or, as some Japanese and a few foreign observers saw them, taken out of context or mistranslated, is not for us to say. We will probably never know for sure just what the men who made the comments really meant. What we can say, however, is that blanket generalizations about one group of people being lazier or less skilled than another are unfair and invalid. How and why people work the way they do, and the quality of the goods they produce, depend far less on their nationality than on a host of other factors. Some people work hard because the money and the benefits are good, and slack off if their job is lousy. The state of the economy influences how many people work and how hard. A company that's proud of its products and is the world or national leader in the manufacture of that product tends to produce hard-working, dedicated workers, and so do companies trying fiercely to catch up; companies and businesses ready to go down the tubes find it very difficult to motivate their workers. How much training, skill, and experience a worker has also determine how hard or capable a worker he or she is. No one ethnic or racial group is superior to any other, neither in intelligence, taste, ability, nor motivation. Culture plays a large role in conditioning a worker to adopt and accept a certain work style, but people are people, and though many Japanese like to believe they are somehow different from everyone else because their culture is so different — a dubious characterization that is unfortunately repeated and accepted over and over again by foreigners who do not know them — they have the same talents and deficiencies, the same successes and failures, the same energy and sluggishness that we and all others have. While some Japanese may not want to admit that they, too, have unproductive, unmotivated, and unhappy workers (the journalist who worked on the assembly line is proof of the latter), the truth of the matter is that, being human, they do. And worse, they also have, as we do, their share of top-level company executives who take bribes, bilk stockholders, evade taxes, and get sentenced to prison.

Similarities aside, there are other notable differences between working conditions in Japan and the U.S. that bear mentioning. One is the salaries of company presidents. Japanese workers receive salaries that are roughly on a par with what American workers receive, but when it comes to the company presidents, ours are paid infinitely more — sometimes astronomically more — than their Japanese counterparts. A recent survey by a Japanese research institute found that Japanese company presidents who manage very large firms get paid an average of $377,950 a year; in the U.S., managers of similar-sized companies get an average of $1.2 million a year.[4]

Another thing that sets Japanese business apart is the relatively low unemployment in Japan; it now stands officially at around 2.3 percent, compared to around 7 percent in 1992 in the United States. Some forecasters believe that the figure will rise over the next few years if there is increased competition from other Asian industrial nations, as Japan continues to switch from an industrial economy to a high-tech service one, and as its labor unions become more demanding.

But for the moment, at least, most of Japan's working age population keeps busy. One reason for the low unemployment rate is the lifetime employment policy of the major companies. Few people quit a job in those companies even if they don't like it or if it's not doing anything for their careers. Few Japanese who work for large firms (especially senior-level executives) care to risk giving up the regular salary increases, prestige, pensions, subsidized housing, expense accounts, and automobiles that come with many lifetime positions. Without the company, a top-level Japanese's self-esteem as well as his livelihood is gone.

Another reason for the low unemployment is that the Japanese society is hard on losers, and social workers tend to emphasize finding work and a place to live as opposed to offering welfare handouts. Writers on Japanese affairs point out, however, that if the statistics were honestly presented, the official unemployment rate would be higher. It has been suggested, for example, that the labor ministry defines the unemployed as anyone who has not worked at all, not even for an hour. But hiring halls regularly employ day laborers of all kinds, from cooks to construction workers, and these part-time workers go on the books as employed, even though they are let go after a day's work and thus are clearly not employed in the strict sense of the definition. In Japan, many other people work part-time, for only a few hours a week, and they, too, are listed among the employed, along with farm laborers who do not get paid at all. Many of these people leave the labor force, but they rarely show up on the official lists as unemployed, simply because they had once been employed.[5]

There is also a lot of needless employment in Japan, according to some observers. Some of it smacks of the old joke about it taking two people to change a light bulb: one to screw in the bulb and another to hold the ladder. One writer mentions a drum of fuel oil that, according to union rules, requires three employees to move it; it sits around for days if only two workers are available and gets moved only when the third man is put on the job. Another story mentions a tobacco warehouse that employs 130 people when only 100 are needed, and a telephone company office that uses a dozen workers to do a job that is routinely handled by two workers on a similar private-sector line.[6] Some large companies have more top-level managers than they need, men that their colleagues refer to caustically as "window starers." But again, we in the U.S. are not always good examples when it comes to padding payrolls. Some of our labor unions have pushed through rules that, supposedly to ensure safety in the workplace, require companies to hire more people than are necessary to do a job (a practice we for years have called featherbedding); some employees in both the public and private sector even manage to get paid for not showing up for work (we call that paying for a no-show).

Although unemployment is low in Japan, where it does exist, it is as unpleasant as it is in the United States. Tokyo's Sanya district, where the day laborers are hired, is a place where a foreign visitor realizes that even in prosperous Japan no work means a tough life. Sanya is known as Japan's "black hole" because it is where thousands of gangsters, vagrants, and people on welfare hang out, warming themselves when it is cold at barrels full of burning newspapers. Many of these people are looking for work, and they crowd into the job centers early every morning to compete for the handful of low-paying construction jobs. It is estimated that nearly a hundred people die every year on Sanya's streets; those who die in the cold of winter are called "tunas," a reference to the frozen tunafish found in Tokyo's central fish market.[7]

On a more pleasant note, Japanese workers and their families do something else that we do not do especially well: save money. Japan has a relatively high household savings rate, between 15 and 18 percent, compared to a rate of a little better than 6 percent in the U.S. Their reasons for putting money aside are the same as ours: protection against illness and damage to their property, for retirement, children's education, to buy cars and household necessities, for recreation, and, their biggest dream, for land or a house.

Japanese families do pay a good deal more than we do for food, apartments, and just about everything else they need — Tokyo and Osaka are the most expensive cities to live in in the world — but they are not reluctant to buy all the gadgets, appliances, and the latest electronic equipment on the market. Almost 100 percent of the households have color televisions; more than 60 percent have stereos and VCRs; 76 percent have cars; and more than 20 percent even have pianos jammed in a corner in apartments which, like the one Hiroshi and Atsuko Miyawaki lived in in Japan, have been often referred to as "rabbit hutches."

Japan's industrious work force, as antlike and robotlike as it sometimes seems to us, has been responsible for all the goods and services that the Japanese — indeed, Americans too — enjoy, and the country's enviable prosperity. Unfortunately, some Americans tend to shrug off the Japanese workers' drive, either because they don't like to be upstaged by a nation that we defeated in World War II or because they see Japan as a threat to us. Sometimes, too, we hear people say that the Japanese are mere imitators, that they don't have any original ideas, and that whatever they've achieved in technology and electronics they've taken from somebody else. Somebody has even suggested that the Japanese method of study forces students to use the left sides of their brain, which enables a person to memorize and calculate, and that teachers neglect the right side, which allows us to think creatively and originate things. That's a fairly simplistic answer, and to say that the Japanese know only how to imitate is a most unfair characterization. If patent applications are any indication of a nation's creative powers, then Japan has done rather well: some 40 percent of the applications filed worldwide every year are from Japan. Japanese artists who turn out paintings, sculpture, and wood-block prints are creating; so, too, are Japanese poets and novelists, potters and weavers, actors, dancers, and fashion designers.

An imitation is a reproduction, a copy, something that slides easily out of, say, a Xerox machine. When the Japanese take something that's already been discovered (and don't assume that they always do, given that a Japanese scientist little known in the West played an important role in the development of television), whether it be an idea or an invention, they usually don't just make a copy of it. They carefully assess it first. If it's an idea that's never been put to practical use, they figure out how to do that; if it has, they try to make or use it better; if it's something that their culture is unfamiliar with, they adapt it. This process takes intelligence, creativity, intuition, and patience. Anyone who is familiar with Japanese products — and it's hardly likely that anyone isn't — has to agree that quality, which is not imitated but created, is their hallmark. The Japanese didn't invent electronics or cars or steel, but they make superior examples of each. Perhaps it is an inner spirit that drives them to search for more efficient ways of building something that is better, or perhaps it's just necessity. There's no question that they take great care in everything they do, whether it's building a television set or putting on a kimono. If you go to a luxury hotel or an inn in Japan, you might see women on their hands and knees snipping the grass of a lawn with manicure scissors or cleaning rubber treads on stairs with tiny knives. And then there's perseverance. The Japanese love to tell stories of their ancient swordsmiths, who learned how to achieve the best temperature for forging the steel only after many years of apprenticeship. Once, a young apprentice decided to shortcut the process by placing his hand close to a white-hot blade to check the temperature. His master drew a knife from his sash and slashed off the apprentice's hand. So much for easy solutions, such as copying something. Hard work and careful thought are really what are behind Japan's quality goods.

9

Even Workaholics Take Time Out

$\mathcal{E}$ ven though they work longer hours and have less vacation time than we do, the Japanese, contrary to what you may have heard, like to play as much as Americans. As we've pointed out, more Japanese are paying attention to leisure time these days. They watch television and videotapes (probably the favorite pastime in Japan); flock to baseball games, horse races, and parades; play tennis and golf and all manner of games; ski, jog, and work out; go to the ballet; go to see traditional forms of theater involving puppets or masks; eat out in restaurants; take advantage of more than a dozen national and other holidays; and travel just about everywhere. In any given year, nine or so million Japanese go overseas as tourists, with the U.S. the prime destination, followed by Korea and Hong Kong. New York City, San Francisco, Los Angeles, and Hawaii are the most popular Japanese tourist spots in the U.S. By contrast, about 3.5 million foreigners visit Japan every year, about a million and a half of them tourists. At home, the Japanese garden, raise miniature trees in pots, arrange flowers, fold paper into

114

lovely shapes, and participate in traditional ceremonies that involve just about everything from burning incense to serving tea to celebrating the first blooming of cherry blossoms.

Some of Japan's leisure time activities are, as you can see, exactly like ours — including the non-activity of just being a couch potato, which has caught on recently as many people have found they are too busy to do anything but nothing. The Japanese even use our phrase *couch potato,* but the habit of hanging around the house eating junk food, listening to music, and watching American and Japanese TV shows is generally referred to by critics as "passive and reclusive type of leisure." Teenagers who spend their time this way are referred to as *go-mo,* which means "Five Nothings." The "Five Nothings" are the qualities, according to some older Japanese, that Japanese youths lack: appreciation of tradition, seriousness, toughness, industriousness, and selflessness.

Couch potatoes aside, many leisure activities the Japanese enjoy are distinctly Japanese. One example may be found in their holidays. Like us, they observe New Year's Day, but it is a time for dressing up, repapering walls, flying kites, paying off debts, and visiting shrines, temples, and relatives. In January, too, there is Adults' Day, which honors young people who have reached the age of twenty, the voting age. National Foundation Day, on February 11, celebrates the accession to the throne of the first emperor, Jimmu. Vernal Equinox Day, in March, observes the coming of spring. Golden Week, beginning on April 29, is a series of back-to-back springtime holidays that includes Constitution Day, May 3, in honor of the country's peaceful, postwar constitution, and Children's Day, May 5, when offspring are honored. In September, there is Respect for the Elderly Day on the fifteenth, as well as Autumnal Equinox Day, to observe the first day of fall and pay respects to the dead. October 11 is Sports Day, and November includes Culture Day and Labor-Thanksgiving Day, a day devoted primarily to rest and relaxation. Emperor Akihito's birthday, a national holiday, is on December 23. In addition, the Japanese have various festivals, among them a flower festival on April 8 to celebrate the birth of Buddha and the Shichi-Go-San (which means seven-five-three) Festival in November, during which parents take their seven-year-old girls, five-year-old boys, and three-year-old boys and girls to shrines to thank the gods for blessings and to pray for the children's healthy growth.

There are some other uniquely Japanese leisure-time and recreational activities, several of which are familiar to many Americans. Many of them, aside from being quite old, are full of ritual and meaning.

In the theater, the Japanese watch three traditional forms of drama: Kabuki, No, and Bunraku. Kabuki stories revolve around historical and domestic themes and are acted almost exclusively by men, who play the female roles as well. Kabuki actors, whose fathers or other male relatives were also in Kabuki, try to be even more feminine than real women, and in doing so they portray the ideal, and the stereotypic, Japanese woman. Some geishas and actresses even study Kabuki actors so that they can be more womanly. No is a more serious form of drama that is backed by drums, flutes, and a chorus. The actors wear false faces and elaborate costumes as they play out stories that are often heavy with history and Buddhist ideas. Bunraku uses life-size costumed wooden puppets that are held and manipulated by puppeteers dressed in black, who are always visible onstage, while a chanter recites the lines.

A Kabuki actor

For spectator sport, along with their beloved baseball, the Japanese have sumo wrestling. Before they start to battle in a clay and sand ring, the two gigantic wrestlers spend a good deal of time bowing, flexing their muscles, sprinkling salt to purify the ring, clapping their hands to get the gods' attention, squirming around, and circling about. The object of the match is to force an opponent out of the ring or get him to touch any part of his body but the soles of the feet on the ground. A match can be over in a flash.

Another uniquely Japanese tournament sport is *kyudo,* "the way of the bow." It is also known as Zen archery, and it is far more than merely shooting an arrow at a target. Zen archery is an art, a religious experience, a form of meditation, a concentrator of physical energy, and a search for perfection. Shooters must go through a series of meticulous steps that dictate how to hold the bow, position the arrow, and breathe. After bowing formally to the target and with feet spread apart an arrow's length, the archer is ready to shoot. This is how the final moment has been described:

> *At full extension, step six, there is no strain. The lines of the body are straight, and all the energies are balanced. . . . Bow, archer, arrow, and target are now as one. This ineffable moment continues for eight to ten seconds. Then, suddenly, like a drop of water that has been gathering and then falls, the arrow flies — unintentionally — toward the mark.*[1]

Some people have likened Zen archery to martial arts such as karate, a method of self-defense that relies on kicks and punches, and kendo, which is the Japanese art of fencing with bamboo swords. But unlike karate and kendo, in *kyudo,* there is no opponent but oneself, and there is no violence. Moreover, because a person doing Zen archery practices against an immovable target, he or she has no one to blame for any mistakes that may be made. *Kyudo* is one more example of the way the Japanese focus their attention on a goal, and of the pains they take to achieve it.

Other Japanese leisure-time activities, such as ikebana, bonsai, origami, and *kodo,* demand the same kind of attention.

Ikebana is the art of flower arranging. Just as Zen archery is more than firing off an arrow, ikebana is more than just sticking some flowers into a vase to decorate a room or a table. Ikebana

An ikebana arrangement

arrangements are used to decorate, too, but they are truly works of art, like paintings or sculpture. Form and balance are most important in the arrangements, and no two arrangements are alike. Each flower and grass is associated with a month or season and also has some special meaning. Acacia, for instance, may mean friendship; bamboo, loyalty; columbine, fickleness; gardenia, purity; pansy, friendship; tulips, kindness; wisteria, welcome. Thus, when a work of ikebana is finished, it is not only symbolic of, say, a month or a time of year, but it stimulates a feeling of that month or season, and creates a mood that links people to nature, something very important to the Japanese. Ikebana's flowers are substitute words and phrases — a way the Japanese communicate without speaking.

Bonsai is another kind of substitute — one that uses miniature trees to symbolize the larger world of nature. Because Japan is a relatively small country, it is very difficult for people to get away from the crush of crowds, no matter where they go. Through bonsai, trees that normally grow tall and full are specially pruned and trained to grow small enough to fit into trays and pots, thereby enabling people to bring nature into their homes and backyard gardens. A collection of bonsai can make parts of an apartment or garden look like a miniature forest. And, like ikebana, bonsai trees suggest rather than making a firm statement, again, something the Japanese prefer in their language and in almost all of their art. Many Japanese spend a good deal of time propagating, dwarfing, and caring for bonsai, and as leisure activity, it not only helps the Japanese forget about work but it creates another world for them and puts them in a peaceful mood.

Origami is another art form and hobby; it involves folded paper instead of flowers and trees. Throughout Japan people of all ages can turn scraps of paper into all sorts of objects and shapes that go way beyond the folded paper planes we've all tossed around. Even shopkeepers carefully fold paper around goods they've sold, hiding a loaf of bread, say, in a paper kite, or a book in a paper hat. Paper is also widely used in Japan to make screens, called shoji; umbrellas that are more decorative than functional; fans for formal attire, to cool oneself, as a prop in plays and dances, and even as a symbol of authority, as when it's carried by a sumo referee.

Another of these unique art forms that play an important part in helping the Japanese relax is *kodo,* an ancient ceremony in which one burns incense not only for its aroma but to help one meditate, form pleasant mental images, and even to improve memory and judgment. The Japanese refer to their *kodo* ceremony as "the hearing of incense." This means they "listen" to it, and try to find messages and inspiration in the various fragrances. In a *kodo* ceremony, a group of people, led by a grand master, pass around smoking containers and try to guess the ingredients that make up a particular blend, and perhaps try to compose a poem from the "messages" they receive from the aromas.

Games are also popular forms of leisure activity, as they are here. Japanese kids and adults play many of the board and card games that we do, along with traditional ones, like mah-jongg, which is of Chinese origin and is played with elaborately painted tiles that are drawn and discarded until a player wins, and go, a game that is as intricate as chess and is played with black-and-white stones on a checkered board. Many of the traditional games, especially go, do not appeal to Japanese teens, who seem to prefer video and computer games and the pool tables found in many centers.

Finally, no discussion of Japanese leisure activities is complete without mentioning three other forms of relaxation. While they aren't serious art forms like some of the others we've talked about, they are, nonetheless, quite popular among the Japanese. They are *karaoke, pachinko,* and *onsen. Karaoke* is singing along with tape-recorded music, and Japanese teens are really into it.

They do *karaoke* at parties and in youth centers, and even study it in special "*karaoke* high schools" that are run by tape manufacturers.

Pachinko, a mechanical game, is a costly form of entertainment. And, like playing slot machines, it can be addictive. *Pachinko* can best be likened to vertical pinball. The *pachinko* machines stand up on end rather than as tables, and players face the glass-enclosed tracks and channels for steel balls. (The name of the game comes from the *chink* sound of the balls.) Players buy the balls and feed them into the machines, the idea being to send them through high-win channels by pushing buttons and levers, and then collect as many as one can as they pour out. The balls are then turned in for cash credit, or household

Pachinko *machines*

goods and food from a shop that is part of the *pachinko* parlor. To the discomfort of the authorities, *pachinko* has been gaining in popularity, as has a recent version called *pachislot,* which combines the traditional game with a slot machine. Adults and kids spend a lot of time and money each year on *pachinko,* which critics sniff at as "mindless diversion" appropriate for the *go-mo* and for workers too tired after all the hours they put in on the job to do anything else.

Onsen is the Japanese spring bath. The bath has an important place in Japanese culture. People don't take one just to get clean. They soak in tubs at home after work to relax, and they often go to the more than two thousand hot springs, the *onsen,* to soak individually or in groups, looking for cures for everything from bad backs to bad love affairs. (Mixed bathing, incidentally, is not as common as it once was, and men and women have separate baths at the spas.) As with many activities in Japan, bathing in public has its ritual. Foreigners soon learn that it's not acceptable to just jump in with their clothes on, as though entering a swimming pool. The bather must first wash with soap and towel while sitting on a stool; he or she then rinses off with a hand-held shower. Perhaps only in Japan can simple soap and towel cleanse the spirit as well as the body.

10

Crime, Koban, *and the* Yakuza

We've made a lot of how the Japanese differ from us, and how they are the same. And by now, you've probably realized that there are many more similarities than differences, even though some Japanese, caught up in a belief in uniqueness, would deny that.

One more cultural phenomenon we share with the Japanese, unfortunately, is crime. Japan's rate may be far lower than our own, but crime nonetheless exists, and in every form that we know it in the United States: murder, robbery, rape, extortion, bribery, computer fraud, kidnapping, terrorism, arson, counterfeiting, hijacking, serial killing, drug dealing, vote buying, burglary, and assaults — and there is even a Japanese version of the Mafia.

A glance at a sampling of headlines from Japanese newspapers gives you an idea of the kinds of crimes the police have had to deal with: "Man Kills Son During Argument Over Stereo," "Woman, Mad Over Hair-Clipping, Kills Husband," "Grandmother's Enemy Arrested for Robbery," "Three Hurt When

124

Gangster Fires Pistol at Police," "Former Judge Gets One Year in Jail for Demanding Sexual Favors," "Police Say Dentist Used Poison on Girl's Teeth," "Wooer of Wealthy Women Arrested for Swindling," "Son Fractures Skull of General," "Gas Station Hit for Six Million Yen," "Company President Kills 3 Construction Workers With Gun and Swords," "Robber Burns Down House, Stabs Woman," "Knife-Wielding Addict Kills Four, Wounds Three in Osaka," "Shimonoseki Police to Probe Report of Drug Use by Police," "Woman Throws Self, Two Sons into Path of Train," "Kimono Slasher Caught in Osaka," "Underwear Thief Nabbed, Knifes Way Free," "Drug User Takes Five Hostages," "Fugitive Plays Tag With Tokyo Police," "Woman Sentenced for Starving Baby," "Another Passing-Fiend Murder."

Sound familiar? Except for the names of some of the cities, most of the headlines could have appeared in your local newspaper. Yes, there is plenty of crime in Japan and, according to the Ministry of Justice and other agencies, the number of criminal offenses has been increasing since 1979. There are many reasons for the rise, but in these times most are probably tied to the sluggish economy: emotional distress and frayed tempers caused by job and profit losses as businesses fail, investments go bad, and construction projects are postponed or halted.

But let's put that into perspective. Japan is still, at this writing, in pretty good shape economically; and it is still among the safest, most law-abiding countries in the world. People who forget their briefcases, coats, umbrellas, even wallets and purses, almost always find them just where they left them; traffic signals are obeyed, even when the streets are deserted; fare beating in the subways is almost unheard of; merchants hardly ever rip off a foreign visitor. Street mugging, so common in our major cities, almost never occurs in Japan, and a person can be comfortable walking most streets and parks alone, even late at night. The murder rate is 1.5 per 100,000 people, compared with nearly 8 per 100,000 in the U.S. Firearms and other weapons are severely restricted. Much of the larceny that goes on in Japan is petty — shoplifting and bicycle theft are among the biggest headaches — and drugs are nowhere near as widespread as in the United States. So overall, Japan's crime rate remains relatively low compared to ours and to that in many other countries.

Much of the credit for the relative peace and quiet must go to the Japanese people. Their natural restraint, family-instilled values, and their need to conform to society's expectations (along with a healthy dose of fear of authority) make them think twice before they do something their relatives and their culture disapprove of. Credit also has to go to the police force of more than 250,000, which gives the country a high ratio of police to citizens compared to that of most industrial nations.

Law enforcement is also helped significantly by a unique network of *koban,* or police boxes, that are located every few blocks in the cities. There are some 15,000 *koban* and substations in Japan, each maintaining close contact with police headquarters and patrol cars. The police who staff the *koban* know virtually everyone in the neighborhood around the box, which means they are especially alert when they see someone they don't know. A foreigner or new Japanese family moving into the neighborhood often gets a personal visit from the *koban* cop, who hands out a questionnaire that will provide all the information the police need to know about the resident. Because of the police box system, it generally takes the police an average of five minutes and fifty-two seconds (the National Police

A koban

Agency is quite precise about this time) to reach the scene of a crime after an emergency call.

Moreover, the training and investigative skills of the police are commendable. Candidates must take rigid examinations, and only one in seven is accepted. Almost all the high-ranking police brass has graduated from Japan's prestigious Tokyo University. In one recent year, the police solved 97 percent of the 1,700 murders and 55 percent of all thefts. In the U.S., police might solve 73 percent of the murders, and 17 percent of the thefts.[1]

The police are not only efficient but are also generally well liked and respected by the public, something that is not always true in the United States. As a Japanese newspaper once put it, the police "enjoy the status of the neighborhood uncle." Local cops patrol the streets on ordinary bicycles with no gears; they hold public hearings and send out questionnaires to find out how they're doing; they take drunks home, and will often walk you to your destination when you ask directions; they entertain the neighborhoods by playing in brass bands. They also have wide discretionary powers and resolve a lot of incidents themselves, out of court. So, along with fast detection and apprehension, the police can boast of fast disposal of cases — three elements that make for good crime prevention. Here's what one American businessman who lived in Japan for many years had to say about those discretionary powers:

> *When a Japanese policeman stops you and asks, "Where's the fire?" he is really interested. His feeling is that if you are rushing home to put out the fire to save Grandma and the kiddies, you should press on. If you were rushing to save your second set of clothes at your mistress' love nest, you get a ticket for speeding.*
>
> *[Once] I was the guilty party who rear-ended the car in front of me while on my way home in bumper to bumper traffic from a Naval Reserve weekend drill. . . . I was still in my Navy uniform, and I think I was let off easy due to the gold bars, but the policeman, who soon materialized magically at the scene of the accident, was soon suggesting that we all avoid the paper-*

work involved if I would hand over the amount of yen that he determined would straighten out the minor dent in the bumper of the citizen who had the misfortune to have been in front of me. No fuss, no muss, no time wasted, and no lawyers.[2]

Obviously, Japanese police have an advantage over ours in that the country is smaller, with most of the population confined to a few large urban centers. The easily recognizable, "all-Japanese" population also helps, as does the fact that the Japanese people aren't on the move throughout their country as fiercely as Americans are; when people aren't overly mobile, it's easier for the police to keep track of who belongs and who doesn't in the neighborhoods. People also cooperate with the police far more than they do here.

There are prisons in Japan, of course, for both men and women, even for traffic offenders. There are also detention centers and reformatories. Most of them differ in a number of ways from our own penal institutions. A prison for men might have walls so low you could vault over them, because very few inmates try to escape. Although guards are always on watch, they are rarely armed, and carry only nightsticks. The rules are often stricter than in some of our prisons: no smoking, radios, television, or magazines. Prisoners very rarely create disturbances or riot; they bow to their guards, work, study, exercise, and, in general, do their time quietly until they get out. It wasn't always that way in Japan. Before the Meiji Restoration, in 1868, treatment of prisoners was brutal. Anyone accused was considered guilty; prisoners were beaten with bamboo staves, flogged, branded with white-hot knives, and, when the crime was especially serious, executed by decapitation, crucifixion, or public burning at the stake.

Today, the prison administration relies on a system that promotes prisoners to higher grades on the basis of good conduct. As they are promoted, they are allowed to receive more visitors and write more letters. This time-honored carrot-and-stick approach also maintains the peace. When I asked one warden if there were any other reasons why the inmates seemed to be so law-abiding, he replied, "Well, Japanese men are trained from childhood to be obedient to authority, so it comes naturally." But when I suggested that they had to have broken some law for them to have ended up in prison, he smiled and agreed. "Men are also mean and greedy, and if they can get away with something, they'll try that, too." A Japanese prison psychiatrist gave me another reason for the obedience. "Some of these prisons are filled mostly with gangsters, and they can't afford to stay behind bars too long. So they do what they have to do to get back out on the street and back into business as soon as possible."

Women prison inmates attend lectures; work at various trades for eight hours a day; take courses, including English, bookkeeping, and use of the abacus; and participate as a group in activities designed to maintain their connection with traditional Japanese culture — ikebana, tea ceremony, calligraphy, and haiku writing. Much attention is also paid to what's called progressive treatment. Each new grade an offender achieves represents a step toward rehabilitation and "improved behavior." The women begin by living in unlocked "community rooms" and are allowed few privileges. Later, they move into single rooms and are given more privileges. When they reach the uppermost grade, they are allowed to stay in a small house where they can cook, perhaps put on a kimono, and "live just like ordinary citizens," according to one prison warden.

As structured and efficient as the Japanese prison system is, and although its goal is to ease the offender's reentry into society, prison time is hard, no matter the country, and so, too, is readjustment to life outside. In Japan, with its ordered society and firm traditions, life outside prison can be quite difficult for a former inmate. For a woman, from whom society demands so much, being an ex-convict is to be branded an outcast, damaged goods. Some manage to make a new life, and even to hide their past. But generally, no matter how much a woman who has done time in Japan repents or improves, the shame that she has brought to her family, friends, and neighborhood is not always easily forgotten. If she isn't married, chances are she'll have a hard time finding a spouse; the work she'll do for the rest of her life won't ever be very meaningful; and if she ever does have children, they, too, will have to bear the shame, and life won't be easy for them, either.

Japan has capital punishment, in the form of death by hanging. The number of prisoners on death row is not made public, as it is in the United States. It's estimated that perhaps two dozen or so people are awaiting death in Japan, compared to some 2,500 in the U.S., a figure that is probably higher than all the people Japan has executed in the last fifty or more years. Neither is the date of an execution made public in Japan. When an offender is condemned to death, that is generally the last his relatives will see or hear of him or her. Occasionally, appeals are taken up on behalf of someone on death row, as in the celebrated case of Sadamichi Hirasawa, who was on death row for some forty years for allegedly fatally poisoning twelve bank clerks in a 1948 bank robbery. Hirasawa, who protested his innocence and vowed to prove it even if he had to live to be 110, was believed to be the world's longest occupant of a death row cell. He appealed to the Japanese Supreme Court for commutation of his death sentence on several occasions, but his appeals were turned down each time. An association to help Hirasawa was also unsuccessful in winning a parole. Hirasawa died a few years ago in prison, of natural causes, at the age of ninety-five.

When an execution actually takes place, it is done without publicity. Sometimes even the condemned prisoner does not know when he is to be executed; he often finds out only when a guard shows up at his cell to escort him to the gallows chamber. Relatives, who sometimes are allowed to visit the condemned criminal, usually learn that the sentence has been carried out when the executed man's ashes arrive at their home or when they are called and asked to come and pick them up at the prison. As in the United States, the death penalty in Japan has been challenged as unconstitutional; the country's Supreme Court has ruled that it is not.

Another crime-related institution the Japanese share with us is a gangster underworld, in their case, the *yakuza,* which is Japan's crime syndicate. Numbers are difficult to obtain, but it's estimated that there are about three thousand *yakuza* organizations, with a total membership of around one hundred thousand. The different groups have names like Yamaguchi-gumi, the largest of the gangs, Miyawaki-gumi, and Kawachika-gumi. The gangs, which can be as violent as any in the United States, rake in billions of dollars from illegitimate businesses such as loan sharking, gambling, gun running, extortion, drugs, and prostitution, as well as from legitimate businesses, including real estate, golf courses, and construction projects.

Yakuza often cover their bodies from head to toe with gaudy tattoos, and when one of them violates a gang's rules, he gets his little finger cut off. Every so often, the police conduct massive raids and arrest the gangsters for some illegal activity. But it's not a crime to be a member of a *yakuza* gang, and many gangsters parade around quite openly, untouched by the police as long as they stick to their underworld haunts and don't engage in violence. Occasionally, *yakuza* have worked for the police, fighting radical groups that were disrupting society. Many *yakuza* even proudly display their gang logos on brass plates tacked to the doors of their fancy offices and show up at various company board meetings, either to make trouble or to deal.

All that may soon change. A new anti-gang law, The Statute Relating to Prevention of Unjust Acts by Crime Syndicates, designates the gangs as violent organizations, and gives the police new powers to crack down on their activities. But the *yakuza* protested — with lawsuits, street marches, and intimidation. One gang leader argued that the new law violated his constitutional rights to choose his own profession and deprived him of his right to earn a living. Another said that the Yamaguchi-gumi was a Robin Hood band that sided with the weak and the poor. Still another admitted his organization engaged in gambling but said that, as professionals, gang members were punished if they carried guns, and that the drug dealing they did helped Japan because it prevented a lot of foreign drug dealers from overrunning the country. Some *yakuza* even displayed characteristic Japanese courtesy. "We accept the anti-mob law with reverence," said one. "We hope the police will execute the new law with prudence," said another.[3] It's hard to imagine an American gang member behaving that way, but, once again, culture dictates behavior.

Culture also lies behind the Japanese attitude toward suicide, a grave social problem, but also, in the view of many, an unpunishable crime. Suicide in Japan has a long history. Heroes and heroines take their lives regularly in Japanese literature, either alone, or together in love suicides. You've undoubtedly heard of hara-kiri, the Japanese form of ritual suicide in which a person disembowels himself or herself with a short sword. Samurai and government officials were bound to commit hara-kiri when they disgraced themselves or committed some crime; sometimes, after the self-inflicted wound was made, an executioner finished the job by cutting off the person's head with a sword.

Hara-kiri as a decree became obsolete in the 1800s, but suicide to save personal honor and wipe away disgrace did not. That is not to say that Japanese do not commit suicide for the same reasons that people in other countries do. Hundreds of executives and others with financial difficulties kill themselves in Japan every year, as do elderly people depressed over illnesses, teenagers who feel pressured to live up to high expectations or who just do not feel good about themselves, as well as widows and widowers left alone.

But in Japan, because honor is all-important, and because suicide has long been regarded as an honorable way to cleanse dishonor from a person's soul, it is not uncommon for people to kill themselves for reasons that are alien to most Americans. Presidents of Japanese companies who have led their firms to ruin have apologized in public, then killed themselves; mothers have leapt to their deaths in front of trains, often taking their infant children with them, both to atone for being unfit mothers and to save the children from living with some disgrace they may have heaped on the family.

Some glaring examples of honorable suicide occurred during World War II. We've mentioned the kamikaze pilots who dove their bomb-laden planes into American warships in the Pacific. Even worse were the suicide attacks that occurred on the island of Saipan, when three thousand Japanese soldiers, armed with sticks and bayonets and wishing to die honorably, charged recklessly into barrages of American machine-gun fire and were all killed. Many of the soldiers had been wounded earlier, and had come out of hospitals in bandages and on crutches to participate in the mass suicide. Civilians on Saipan also committed suicide en masse. In one of the war's most horrendous incidents, waves of men and women, with babies in their arms, leapt from cliffs into the sea, preferring death to the disgrace of surrender. The suicides went on for three days, and when they ended, only a thousand people were left of the island's original 30,000 inhabitants.

We opened this chapter by suggesting that the Japanese were probably more similar to us than different, and that one of the cultural phenomena they share with us is crime. But if suicide can be called a crime, in the matter of ritual suicide — which is actually violence directed against oneself — the Japanese are distinctly Japanese.

Part Three

U.S.—Japanese Relations

11

What Americans Think of the Japanese

The following comments made by American visitors about the Japanese, collected by a Japanese educational research institute, are representative of the "intercultural communication block" that many foreigners feel when confronted with a Japanese person. You can call them misunderstandings.

- It is irritating and a waste of time that they don't say yes or no, or what they really think, clearly and directly. They seem immature and cowardly. It's difficult to grasp main points.
- It is irritating and a waste of time that they don't exchange ideas but spend too much time on formal greetings. Too much consciousness of form and very little of content.
- They ask too many personal questions, such as age, marital status, number of children, and too earthy questions about sex, which is very embarrassing.

- They treat us as if we were fools; they seldom explain first, but often say, "You foreigners can't understand." The use of "can't" is very insulting.
- They don't express their own opinions but keep silent in public as if they were stupid. As individuals, they are extremely polite and kind, but in groups they're unbelievably rude, and also they're indifferent to other groups in the Japanese society. There is terrifying conformity, no individuality or originality.
- It takes time to get an answer to the simplest question. It is ambiguous who is the decision maker and who is responsible for what, and so who should be accused when a contract is not observed?
- There isn't any discussion in the true sense of the word. Their opinions are sorted out ahead of time, and prearrangements made, and so the "discussion" is just a formality.[1]

Critical comments like these about Japan by foreigners (and we are, of course, included in that category) have become increasingly common these days as Japan grows mightier, and as more and more Japanese deal with Americans. They and their wares seem to be everywhere. Thousands of Japanese live here, and many more thousands visit every year; some 80,000 come to the U.S. in a year just to study. In 1974, there were sixty Japanese restaurants in New York City; today there are more than six hundred.[2] Japanese cars and cameras and electronic equipment have shoved once-dominant American products aside; lobbyists hired by hundreds of Japanese government agencies, industries, and trade associations patrol Washington, D.C., trying to influence legislation and regulations; neon signs advertising Japanese-made products glow high over Times Square; and millions of Japanese yen finance some 80 percent of the studies on U.S.–Japanese relations at American universities and research institutions.[3]

While a majority of Americans admire Japan's industrial and technological achievements, the high quality of its products, and the diligent work styles of the Japanese, many Americans believe the Japanese are trying to buy up America and turn it into a colony, that they crave our oil, wood, tuna, minerals, and all the other natural resources they don't have, that they want to dominate all of Asia, that they're paying us back for dropping atomic bombs on them in World War II, that they want to accomplish what they didn't in that war, that is, win. They have been called greedy, untrustworthy, unfair traders, slave drivers (by their American employees), and a threat. They have been blamed for America's economic downturn and for its high unemployment. Some of our leaders have called for boycotts of Japanese products and for protectionist laws that would exclude many Japanese products. Not only have the Japanese been verbally bashed, but their cars have been literally bashed by angry, sledgehammer-wielding, U.S. autoworkers who have lost their jobs because Americans like Japanese cars.

Indeed, recent polls tell us that Americans have turned increasingly negative about Japan: a Roper Report in 1991 found that 43 percent of Americans regarded Japan a close ally, down from a previous 63 percent; a Times/Mirror Center study in 1992 reported that 31 percent of Americans felt that Japan, among all countries, posed the greatest danger to the U.S.; two years before, only 8 percent of Americans felt that way.[4]

Perhaps what irritates, and angers, Americans more than anything else about the Japanese is their investment in prime U.S.

real estate and businesses, the trade barriers they have thrown up against U.S. goods, and the fact that Japanese cars have taken over some 30 percent of our auto market. The investment issue is an especially galling one to some Americans because large chunks of some of our most prized and visible assets have gone to the Japanese: Rockefeller Center, the skyscraper head-quarters of Exxon and Mobil, the Tiffany Building and the Algonquin Hotel in New York City; hotels and golf courses in Hawaii and California; the Seattle Mariners baseball team; and segments of the entertainment industry in Hollywood.

Are the angry accusations and negative perceptions accurate? Are they fair? Are any of them inspired by racism? By envy?

Some are, some are not.

It is true that the Japanese usually place the interests of their country and their companies first in everything they do. That is not unusual or wrong for any country, and for a small one with limited resources it is both understandable and essential. Yes, the Japanese have not always played fair with their trading partners, but neither have we. Yes, the Japanese may make it hard for us and others to sell rice to them at a low price, even when they have a shortage of it and what they do grow is priced ridiculously high. Our apples and oranges have a tough time getting into Japan, as does Chinese and Korean silk, which is far cheaper than Japanese silk; our companies don't generally have the same freedom to set up in Japan as theirs have over here; and often when new, competitive American products come on the market, they don't make it into the complicated Japanese distribution system. Sometimes the excuses a few Japanese give for restricting or banning imported goods seem a bit contrived: the quality and taste of imported rice is unsuited to Japanese taste buds; pharmaceuticals are inadequately tested (by Japanese standards); American cars are either inferior or too big; imported silk isn't necessary because kimonos are not as popular as they used to be; imported beef is full of chemicals and doesn't suit Japan's traditional diet anyway; processed lumber doesn't meet size and quality requirements (raw logs do, however). The list of excuses, many of them in the category of cultural obstacles, seems endless.

On the other hand, Americans must, to put it bluntly, grow up when it comes to Japan. We have paid so much attention to the trade dispute that we tend to forget that Japan is still our best friend in Asia and one of the best we have in the world. Also, it's fair to say that many of our economic woes have nothing to do with the trade imbalance but with our own actions and decisions, such as heavy military spending, emphasis on quick profits while neglecting long-term ones, shabby management practices, our lavish spending habits and reticence to save, and sending production overseas instead of employing American workers — so many of our products are now manufactured in other countries that the now familiar expression "Buy American" is meaningless.

Many of the things we criticize Japan for have to be taken for what they are: competitive responses, steps to protect their own farmers and industries, and, indeed, cultural peculiarities. Here's how Japan's Central Union of Agricultural Cooperatives saw the situation a few years ago:

Beef and citrus represent major sources of income for Japan's small farmers, and have reached 40 percent and 10 percent of domestic production respectively. Japan is about the size of Montana, with only 17 percent of its land arable. The average Japanese farm is 1/150th the size of the average U.S. farm. If

*imports are allowed to increase, they will drive out domestically
produced beef and citrus, which will mean the end of many small
family farms in Japan.*

*Japan's food self-sufficiency is the lowest of all the industrial
countries — less than one-third of its total requirements. Japan
is the largest importer of agricultural and fishery products — a
very risky situation for any country. A country should produce
as much food at home as possible, relying on imports to meet
unsatisfied demand. Japan learned this bitter lesson in 1973
when the U.S. embargoed soybeans (for political reasons having nothing to do with Japan) and created tremendous economic
difficulties.*[5]

Many Americans agree with that view. They've called Japan
bashing sour grapes and hypocrisy, and argue that if American
firms really want to do well in Japan, they have to try harder
and improve the quality of their goods. They point out that
many foreign cars are made in U.S. plants, with American-
made parts, that many Japanese companies contribute heavily
to U.S. charities and foundations, that contrary to what we
believe about Japan buying up America, foreigners — Great
Britain being at the top of the list — own only 5 percent of total
U.S. assets, and that all of the Japanese investment in U.S. real
estate helps rather than hinders us because it pumps money into
our economy.

It is important to know, too, that while Japan has penetrated
our markets quite deeply, and though many of our businesses
don't make it in Japan, including automobile and steel manufacturing, we do sell the Japanese a lot of other goods, American exports to Japan are growing, and many U.S. companies

have done very well by setting up shop on Japan's own turf. We also impose quotas on certain products and have enormous trade surpluses with other countries that could just as well be criticized by those countries. Japan is the second largest foreign customer, after England, of Boeing, which makes airplanes in Seattle. Tons of wheat and wood from our Northwest go regularly to Japan. Japan has been the largest single importer of U.S. agricultural products, buying billions of dollars worth of farm and fishery products annually. Japan also buys a large percentage of the beef that we export, and many U.S. companies — Kodak, Coca-Cola, IBM, Microsoft, Merck, and Baskin-Robbins, to mention just a few — have done well in Japan.

"However scapegoating Japan may play on the election trail," said a recent editorial in *America* magazine,

> *it is the height of geopolitical and economic idiocy. Both Tokyo and Washington know this. Our two economies are joined at the hip. Yes, Toyota and Honda and the rest have captured . . . the U.S. auto market. But nearly 40 percent of those cars are manufactured in places like Smyrna, Tennessee, and Marysville, Ohio. For some 600,000 Americans, Japanese investment here means food on the table. And yes, Tokyo's domestic market has been tougher for American companies to break into than we would like. But since 1988, Japan has moved dramatically away from protectionism, almost doubling its imports from the States. And who can blame the Japanese if they refuse to buy Chevrolets when the wheel is on the wrong side? [The Japanese drive on the left side of the road, and the steering wheel of their cars is on the right.]*[6]

Some have also suggested that Japan bashing stems not from Japan's unfair trading and business practices but from racism. No one seems to care that the English and the Canadians and the Dutch have bought up more American properties than the Japanese, and few Americans are outraged when other countries open banks or sell cars here, but a great hue and cry goes up whenever the Japanese do the same things.

It's hard to say how much, if any, of the anti-Japanese sentiment we hear expressed today is due to racism. Certainly, American citizens of Japanese descent have been the targets of bigotry here over the years. They have been accused of taking jobs away from "real" Americans, they have been denied jobs because of their race, and they have never been allowed to forget Pearl Harbor. Many loyal Japanese-Americans were sent to concentration camps in the United States during World War II, and even now we hear people say the Japanese cannot be trusted because of what their country did to us in that war.

If our criticism of the Japanese is based on racism, then it is wrong and can only breed more mistrust, nationalism, and hatred. In the 1950s, Americans spent a lot of money overseas, just as the Japanese now do here and in other countries. We were called the "ugly Americans" back then by Europeans who envied our wealth and success and hated us for investing in their countries so easily. But our money did a lot for Europe, helping get it back on its feet after a devastating war. In somewhat the same way, we might regard Japan's money as helping America, not hindering it, and we ought to think twice before referring to the "ugly Japanese."

In the final analysis, we have to understand that the Japanese have reasons for their behavior, just as we do. Their highly organized, communal society is designed to protect the country and the ways of its people. We may not always like what the Japanese do, or how they do it, but the fact remains that that is their way, just as we might do things our way. Given that probably half of all Americans don't know all that much about Japan, it's easy to see why we and other outsiders make generalized, negative statements about the Japanese.

During World War II, Ruth Benedict, the respected American anthropologist, was assigned to study Japanese culture and behavior so that we'd have a better understanding of our then enemy. Her words hold true today:

> *One of the handicaps of the twentieth century is that we still have the vaguest and most biased notions, not only of what makes Japan a nation of Japanese, but of what makes the United States a nation of Americans, France a nation of Frenchmen, and Russia a nation of Russians. Lacking this knowledge, each country misunderstands the other. We fear irreconcilable differences when the trouble is only between Tweedledum and Tweedledee, and we talk about common purposes when one nation by virtue of its whole experience and system of values has in mind a quite different course of action from the one we meant. We do not give ourselves a chance to find out what their habits and values are. If we did, we might discover that a course of action is not necessarily vicious because it is not the one we know.*[7]

Remember that when you hear someone say — as the respondents did in the comments with which we opened this chapter — that the Japanese are rude, ask too many personal questions, or don't speak their minds.

12

What the Japanese Think of Us and Other Gaijin

As we've just seen, when the people of one country look at another, the conclusions they reach are often a mixture of stereotype and fact. The viewers may be influenced by their own cultural prejudices, by personal experiences with the people under scrutiny, by media accounts and portrayals, and by the period in history.

What do the Japanese think of us today, nearly fifty years after World War II? Another question is broader: What do the Japanese think of foreigners in general? Government agencies, professional pollsters, magazines, newspapers, television networks, university think tanks, sociologists, and cultural exchange programs have all tried to answer those questions. As expected with queries of this sort, the answers can reflect love and contempt, envy and admiration.

Let's begin with some comments from the same survey that opened the last chapter. This time, the "intercultural communication block" is reflected in the reactions Japanese have to foreigners.

- They seem childish and unpolished when they pay little attention to others' feelings and say too directly what they think.
- It is unsatisfactory that they don't say a word of thanks later on, as well as at the time they receive a present or some kindness.
- They are not patient enough to sound out individual opinions, but label this or that too quickly, or push their own opinions too strongly.
- They often justify themselves without admitting their faults. It is hard to live in a society where one has to advertise one's ability all the time. Because of extremes of individualism, there is a lack of cooperation resulting in inefficient work.
- Responsibility is clearly assigned to each person, and it is not interchangeable. They seem to be very stubborn and inflexible.
- They discuss thoroughly and act upon the decision in common, although it doesn't reach 100 percent accord. They also conceive of discussion as argument and treat it as a game, which is very embarrassing.[1]

What do you think? How many of the comments are accurate? How many seem off the mark? Which ones reflect cultural differences? Do any of them anger you? Do any of them make you want to improve your attitude?

Over the years, the impressions the Japanese people have of us have shifted back and forth from favorable to unfavorable. Undoubtedly, when World War II broke out, and later when we dropped two atomic bombs on Japan, most Japanese hated America. But when Japan literally lay buried in ashes after its defeat and America helped the country get back on its feet, America was viewed not only as the benevolent conqueror but as a friend, an admired and powerful nation to be thanked and imitated. Back then, and all through the painful rebuilding years, the Japanese felt insecure and inferior to the victorious, wealthy Americans.

Today, most Japanese still regard America as a friend and ally and admire many of our achievements. Diplomatic relations are excellent, and despite the trade problems and the other differences, a majority of Japanese, according to one recent poll, admire our form of government, our leadership role in the world, and our technical accomplishments, freedom of expression, leisure time, respect for family life, and our treatment of women.[2]

This positive picture doesn't mean that some Japanese don't stereotype or criticize us. The comments representing the "intercultural communication block" that we've noted above should make that clear. A lot of Japanese believe Americans eat beef all the time, that we are violent because of all that beef, that everybody in America goes to football games, that our women are too forceful, that our men are weaklings at home because they all do the dishes and the laundry. Some Japanese go further and really bash us, calling us lazy, poorly educated, illiterate, violent, and members of a nation that is either ailing or in a major decline. The reasons behind the bashing are the same as when Americans bash Japan: envy, arrogance, insecurity, resentment, and racism.

Sometimes, Japan's criticisms of us are valid. They tell us we must learn to save more money, improve our schools, try harder to crack their markets, and invest more in scientific research, and indeed we should. The Japanese argue that we always try to tell them what to do, that we complain about their investments in the U.S. out of prejudice, and often this is true. Other times, the criticisms are shots from the hip. One example was the comment by a Japanese politician that American workers are lazy and that 30 percent of them cannot read. The fact is that the U.S. illiteracy rate is around 5 percent, American productivity is higher than Japan's, and Japan lags far behind America in a number of businesses.

One difficulty the Japanese have with us is our diverse culture. America is a mosaic of different ethnic and racial groups; Japan is not. Most Japanese don't say it openly, but many believe that a lot of our problems are due to our lack of racial and ethnic homogeneity. A few tell us how they feel, and when they do, it causes more friction between our two countries because of the way the idea is presented. A few years ago, the then prime minister Yasuhiro Nakasone suggested that our blacks and Hispanics were bringing America down. It wasn't clear whether he meant intellectually or productively, but the remark triggered a storm of outrage from members of those groups, and from other Americans. Nakasone apologized. Another Japanese politician suggested that African-Americans often go bankrupt to avoid paying off their debts, and a justice minister compared foreign prostitutes in Tokyo to American blacks who go to white communities and ruin the neighborhood.

Comments like these not only show insensitivity to our minorities and give us an insight into how some Japanese see us as a nation, but they also say something about how the Japanese perceive anyone who is not Japanese or is otherwise outside their closed system. There is a word in Japan for "outside people": *gaijin,* which applies to all foreigners. Foreign residents must always carry a *gaijin*-card (an alien registration card) with them; if a foreign resident is caught without the card, he or she can be arrested.

There are advantages and disadvantages to Japan's homogeneity. On the plus side, the country has few of the racial problems that we have, management and education becomes easier and more efficient, and life seems generally harmonious. On the other hand, when everyone is technically "the same," the nation loses out because homogeneity stifles diverse thought and forces everyone to conform to one set of rules. Homogeneity also breeds arrogance — one reason why so many Japanese believe that whatever they do, whether it's building computers or cars, or cramming their students full of facts, is unmatched anywhere in the world. Many Japanese feel strongly that they are, indeed, unlike any other people on the planet, and that Westerners can never understand them.

Such firm convictions breed racism and prejudice against any non-Japanese. Some observers have gone so far as to call Japan the most racist country on earth. That's a bit strong, given that there are no national policies that set the races apart, no Ku Klux Klan marches, no skinheads, no terrorizing of ethnic groups, and, with the exception of a few politicians who make unfortunate remarks, no individuals who have made reputations for themselves as racists. Also, Japan's young people adore Michael Jackson and Lionel Richie, along with African-American athletes.

But the deep-seated feeling of superiority that many Japanese have, the belief in their "racial purity," makes them regard others as inferior in both intelligence and competence. Obviously, the main reason for this skewed view is that the Japanese have never dealt directly and regularly, as we do, with large groups of minorities. Not that minorities don't exist in Japan. They do, and despite often-voiced denials, they are often ignored or discriminated against.

Koreans are the largest ethnic group in Japan, numbering about 700,000, and they have been treated shabbily. They are the children and grandchildren of Koreans who were forcibly brought to Japan to work as laborers when Japan occupied their homeland before and during World War II, and many of them cannot get jobs, housing, or bank loans, even though four out of five of them were born in Japan, and speak only Japanese. If a Korean tries to hide his or her ancestry, chances are he or she will be found out, because many companies, as well as many prospective brides, hire private investigators to check out a candidate's background; if the applicants or potential husbands turn out to be Korean, chances are that'll work against them. Moreover, a Korean born in Japan doesn't automatically become a Japanese citizen. While a Korean may become a naturalized citizen, real citizenship is reserved for people of Japanese "blood." (You probably didn't know it, but all Japanese kids can tell you their blood type, and they mention it when they're trying to learn things about themselves and the sort of person they'll get along with. Most American kids probably don't pay much attention to their blood type.)

Unfortunately, however, even Japanese blood doesn't always mean acceptance. Such is the case with the *burakumin,* a group of people who are Japanese but who are still shunned by many of their own countrymen. The *burakumin* (the word means "village people") are the descendants of Japanese who, by family heritage, made a living as tanners of leather, furriers, butchers, and undertakers, occupations considered unclean and low-class.

There are more than a million *burakumin* in Japan, maybe

more, and most of them live in city slums, still working at various "unclean" jobs. Only a handful have been able to rise above their legacy as members of an "untouchable" class. While you could not tell a *burakumin* from an ordinary Japanese, most of them are well-known to companies who hire private investigators to check on applicants' backgrounds, maintain blacklists of *burakumin* family names, and refuse to hire them.

Other Japanese face discrimination, too. We've mentioned the Ainu, Japan's version of our American Indians, an ancient people whose tribal lands were confiscated by rich landowners and whose language and traditions were outlawed. There are also the survivors of the atomic bomb blasts and their descendants, unfortunate Japanese citizens regarded as "damaged goods," a classification that during the war included even Japanese soldiers who were badly wounded, were denied medical care, and, sometimes, were shot by their officers. There are the physically and mentally disabled, who have traditionally been discriminated against in the workplace, even though there are laws against it; the "war orphans," the sons and daughters of Japanese who were left behind in China during the war and who, when repatriated to Japan, are forced to take low-level jobs and are taunted for being Chinese and not Japanese; and the children of mixed Japanese and foreign blood, the *hafu,* or "halfs," who will never fit into Japanese society as they try desperately to live in two cultures.

Given such an attitude toward "outsiders," it is not surprising that many Americans and others who live in Japan also have a tough time fitting in. Someone who found that out was the Irish-Greek writer Lafcadio Hearn, who went to Japan as a correspondent in the late 1800s. He fell in love with the country and wrote a lot about it, praising its culture and its people. He taught English at the University of Tokyo and even became a naturalized citizen. But soon he discovered what it was like to be a foreigner in his adopted country. "His salary was promptly reduced because he was no longer a foreigner," wrote one Westerner who was born and educated in Japan.

> *But the final blow came a few years later, when the Ministry of Education decided that all professors must be Japanese and Hearn was fired. He protested that he had taken out Japanese citizenship. But the administrators shrugged and said, "How can you be Japanese? Your eyes are blue." He died a few years later, a bitter man. End of a great Japanese romance.*[3]

Despite the changes that have occurred in the world and in Japan, when it comes to attitudes toward foreigners, some things haven't changed much since Lafcadio Hearn's stay in Japan. A recent case in point involved the 576-pound American sumo wrestler, Konishiki, whose real name is Salevaa Atisanoe. Konishiki has been wrestling in Japan for more than ten years, and has become one of the country's most admired and talented sports figures. In 1992, after winning a number of important sumo matches, including his third Emperor's Cup, Konishiki and his many fans expected that he would be named a *yokozuna,* or grand champion, sumo's highest rank. But ever since the sport began in Japan in the seventeenth century, no foreigner had ever been awarded the title. The powerful and conservative Japan Sumo Association wasn't about to change that, either. Konishiki was refused the honor, even though other sumo wrestlers with less impressive records had won it.

A national debate erupted over the issue. Critics charged racial discrimination, others insisted Japan was only protecting a tradition, and a few patriots argued that only a Japanese could have the noble spirit, called *hinkaku,* which lives inside top sumo champs. Konishiki entered another important tournament of fifteen matches, and had he won the sumo officials would have had a hard time denying him the grand title. The issue was settled when Konishiki lost four straight matches, proof to some that he lacked the noble spirit. Whether Konishiki lost because of the stress placed on him by the sumo officials' refusal to honor him to begin with, or whether he lacked *hinkaku* is still debated in Japan.

In 1993, however, the argument became meaningless. Chad Rowan, a twenty-three-year-old American who wrestles under the name of Akebono, broke the barrier by becoming the first foreigner recommended for elevation to grand champion.

The sumo controversy is just one more example of how tightly closed Japan's doors remain to foreigners. Another is the fingerprinting issue. Until 1992, all foreigners, including Koreans born in the country, had to be fingerprinted — all the fingers. Many of those forced to submit to the requirement denounced it as discriminatory and insulting and argued that Japan was treating them like suspected criminals. Indeed, the notion that all foreigners were potential crooks was the main reason fingerprinting was made a law in Japan shortly after World War II. (The U.S. orders fingerprints only of foreigners who want to be permanent residents.)

Bowing to pressure, the Japanese Parliament recently revised the alien registration law and eased the fingerprint rules. Permanent foreign residents are no longer fingerprinted. On the surface, the changes are positive, including the new requirement that only one finger need be printed. But critics maintain that the new regulations are but another example of the "Japanese gesture," that is, more show than substance. For one thing, the law still requires that the some 300,000 nonpermanent foreign residents provide their prints. For another, all foreigners, permanent or not, still have to carry the alien card and still face prosecution if they're without it or if they don't report address or job changes. Also, Japan's immigration authorities still make the rules about who gets to become a permanent resident. Some people have lived in Japan for many years, earned a living there, and paid taxes, but are still unable to win permanent status.

It can be argued that the Japanese have every right to make the rules in their own country. And what they think of us is, as we said at the outset, dictated by many things, from cultural prejudices to personal experience. One could also argue that their inward-looking culture and mythological history of sun-gods and sun-goddesses, along with a harmonious and unshakable spirit that has made them a world force, are behind the superiority and the incidents of discrimination.

But whatever it is that drives the way the Japanese feel about foreigners and their own minorities, and how it treats them, is not really as important as how we, as outsiders, should respond. Prejudice and discrimination are wrong in any society, and it behooves us all to speak out against them, no matter where they appear. That is not intruding on a country's sovereignty or trampling on its cultural beliefs, and it just might get the other side to think twice about the way it's treating others.

But before we criticize the Japanese for whatever discrimination some of them may practice, we have to get our own house in order. It's difficult to chide a Japanese employer who refuses to hire a *burakumin* or a disabled person if we don't argue against the way we sometimes discriminate against various immigrant groups, the elderly, and the mentally ill; to criticize neglect of the Ainus if we ignore the plight of our own Indians; to be appalled by the way Japanese-born Koreans are treated if we accept the unequal treatment of American-born blacks.

We should also let our Japanese friends know that we don't think they really are any better than us. They're very good, but not better. We should also wonder whether the Japanese are really all that different from us. Get to know a bit more about their culture and their values. These do, of course, shape their behavior and make it appear different from ours. But not always. Sometimes, when a Japanese argues that he or she is "unique," or shrugs off a question with, "This is Japan," it is nothing more than a convenient way to avoid criticism. It's called the ostrich approach, burying one's head in the sand so as not to face reality. Don't be afraid to tell a Japanese friend something that he or she may not be used to hearing: that he or she is not always so different, that no race or ethnic group has dibs on intelligence and creativity and diligence, that the word *homogeneity* is sometimes just another way of saying *racial purity,* which has distasteful overtones.

We suggested that a people's impressions of others are also influenced by personal experience. If you can offer a reasoned, courteous impression of your Japanese friends when they ask for it, and don't play into stereotypes and myths that set the Japanese apart, you will, it is hoped, be respected.

13

What the Japanese Think of Themselves

Unless you know the Japanese well, it's doubtful you'll ever hear them talk about themselves. They're more apt to ask you questions about yourself — sometimes questions that you might regard as overly personal — because they're very aware that Americans, as a whole, are more open and eager to talk about themselves.

A mistake many of us make when we deal with the Japanese is believing that they never express an opinion and that they beat around the bush a lot. It's true that they're not the most openly opinionated people in the world by any means, and that it often does take them a good deal of time to come up with a straight answer. Those qualities are the result of centuries of isolation and of the culture, religion, and language that all Japanese share. For all their modern ways and their appreciation and imitation of Western style, the Japanese are still very much a tribal people, sometimes suspicious of foreigners, more often still unsure about why we do what we do. That's why they sometimes don't let us into their heads.

But like us, the Japanese take a close look at themselves every so often, and they are quite willing to talk about what they see. They do it at home, and it just takes time for them to feel comfortable discussing their thoughts and feelings with strangers.

Again like us, the Japanese are sometimes pleased with what they see and sometimes not. Many of them say they have a terrible inferiority complex when they compare themselves to the West; others feel they're far superior. Ordinary Japanese often say they and their country are not rich; others insist everyone is doing very well. Some Japanese say they're smarter and work harder than us; others say we've got it all over them. The replies, as in all countries, depend on who's asked the question, their social standing, their education, their age, and their politics, to name the key variables.

From time to time, the Prime Minister's Office and private agencies conduct a nationwide survey "on society and state" or "on the life of the nation" to find out just what the people think about themselves and their country.

Most of the surveys place a good deal of emphasis on gathering statistics about questions such as "Do you believe you live a fulfilling life?," "How do you see your life in the future?," "Are you patriotic?," and "What is your image of present-day Japan?" Perhaps the answers the Japanese people gave to some recent surveys will help you understand how they feel about one another and give you a clue about what they expect and desire.

- Eighty-five percent believe Japan is an economic powerhouse.
- Eighty-three percent believe Japan is scientifically and technologically advanced.

- Nearly 80 percent feel Japan is "pursuing a peace policy."
- Nearly 65 percent believe their personal freedom and rights are guaranteed.
- Fifty-five percent agree that "national life is affluent."
- Fifty-three percent believe that Japan "is highly evaluated abroad."
- Fifty-two percent feel that Japan has a rich culture.
- Asked what terms could best be used to describe the negative aspects of present-day society, "self-centered" came first with 46.3 percent, followed by "irresponsible" (44.9 percent), "restive" (24 percent), and "uneasy and nervous" (16 percent).
- Asked what terms could best be used to describe the positive aspects of society, 72.6 percent said "peaceful," followed by "stable" (33.3 percent), "not hard-pressed" (16 percent), and "dynamic" (11 percent).
- Asked whether Japan was moving in a good or bad direction, 38 percent said good, while 31 percent said bad.
- Asked which opinion they agreed with, "The people should pay more attention to state and social affairs" (a society-oriented approach) or "The people should attach more importance to enriching their personal life" (an individual-oriented approach), 41 percent favored the first, nearly 34 percent the second.
- Asked if they wished to be of any service to society, 54 percent said yes, while 41 percent said they hardly thought of such a thing.
- Asked whether the people should attach more importance to national interests even at the sacrifice of personal benefit or should emphasize their own benefit over that of the entire nation, the respondents were split almost equally.

- Asked which should come first, contribution to the world or Japan's interests, 41 percent replied that Japan should emphasize national interests, and 42 percent said that contribution to the world should be the priority.[1]
- Asked what aspects of their lives they most wanted to emphasize in the future, 31.7 percent selected leisure activities, followed by focusing on their homes (23 percent), and dietary habits (11 percent).
- Forty-six percent said they intended to enjoy a full life now, and 37 percent said they'd concentrate on saving up for the future.[2]
- When asked what they would most want to do, 75 percent of Tokyo ninth graders said, "sleep."

What can you read into these stats? Do any of them surprise you, given what you've been led to believe about the Japanese? Which of the responses appear to indicate a change in what you've read so far about Japanese tradition? Do any of them give you a clue to how the Japanese feel about their country and about other people? Based on the responses, what can you say about the future of Japan?

Let's put how the Japanese feel about themselves and others, and the way they live, and what they want, on a more personal level. At the Children's Museum of Boston, a remarkable exhibit called "Teen Tokyo: Youth and Popular Culture" addresses that question with life-size photographs of typical Japanese teenagers. The captions accompanying the pictures are the replies the teens gave when photographer Bruce Osborn asked them to talk about themselves. When you read the following sampling, ask yourself which teen reminds you of yourself, which one seems most unlike you, which one's life and desires are the same or different from yours.

Yuki Hai, age thirteen. "If I could say anything to adults I'd tell them to leave us alone more. Don't pressure us so much. We'll get there."

Mina Oshima, fifteen. "If I could say one thing to the people of the U.S., I'd tell them not to judge us from just one part, like kimonos, or high tech things like Sony. We're really a mixture of both."

Takumi Sato, thirteen. "If I had one wish, I'd wish for money. I want to make a lot of money."

Shohei Kurosawa, seventeen. "If I could wish for anything, I'd wish for the strongest muscles in the world. . . . I can't wait to be a college student because I'll be able to do whatever I want with my money without getting my parents' permission. They always tell me how I can spend my own money."

Masami Imamura, thirteen. "I like to write. I want to be a novelist someday. My favorite books are *Anne of Green Gables,* the *Diary of Anne Frank,* and *Little House on the Prairie.* Especially Anne Frank. She's my hero. My favorite part of my body is my fingers. I'm always complimented on my fingers; the worst part is my hair; it's too dark and too black."

Izumi Shitanda, seventeen. "My mother and I always disagree on what I should wear. My mother doesn't care what's in or out. She likes clothes that don't stand out. She likes quiet, feminine outfits. I know what styles and colors are good for me."

Masaki Miyoshi, fifteen. "People think I'm a nerd but I'm not. I just like to do things thoroughly. Once, I spent eight hours reading a book in a bookstore. . . . Most people my age waste their time doing nothing. . . . This is when memory and learning ability are best. It's hard to memorize anything when you're older so I've decided to get the hard things done when I'm young. I've decided to spend my time now as efficiently and effectively as possible. Even though I'm only 15, I just passed the national lawyer's exam."

Shinichi Muakata, thirteen. "I want to be a professional baseball player when I grow up. My favorite team is the Hiroshima Carps. I don't like to read books but I do like comic books, especially about baseball."

Yasunari Mochizuki, thirteen. "I want to be a professional sumo wrestler when I grow up. My desire is to be a *yokozuna* [grand champion]. I used to think there was nothing good about being fat. But my mom reminded me that most 13-year-old kids never get to meet all the people I've met through sumo. Once I went to Korakuen Amusement Park with some wrestlers. We were there all day and they bought me all the stuff I wanted. So I guess it wouldn't have happened if I wasn't fat."

14

What the Japanese Don't Say about Themselves

Anytime a group of people takes a close look at itself, there is always the temptation to dilute some of the truth about ugly episodes in the past. Americans are no exception. For years, our history books and movies portrayed Native Americans in an unfavorable light — they were generally the villains while the U.S. Cavalry and the settlers were the good guys. In our unpopular war in Vietnam, atrocities committed by U.S. soldiers were, for a time, glossed over.

The Japanese, too, have often been reticent to face the truth about some events in their history, notably those of World War II. They are very sensitive to how others feel about Japan's belligerent past. The country has scrupulously avoided getting involved in military actions, although it only recently agreed to allow its soldiers to join United Nations peacekeeping forces, provided Japanese restrict their activities to such things as construction projects and medical assistance.

So intent have the Japanese leaders been on erasing their past, however, that the country's Education Ministry have even gone so far as to revise what is written about Japan's role in World War II in some textbooks for young people. They used words like *advance of forces* or *drives* instead of *invasion,* and one text referred to an earlier uprising in Korea against tyrannical Japanese rule as a "riot by violent mobs." Textbooks also deleted the number of Koreans — more than 700,000, according to some accounts — who were used as forced labor during the war. Another textbook used a passive construction to take the onus off the Japanese, saying: "Because of an explosion on the railway, the Japanese Army began fighting with the Chinese Army." The text didn't explain that the explosion was caused by Japanese soldiers destroying the railroad. Atrocities committed by Japanese troops in China that left hundreds of thousands of Chinese dead are sometimes deleted from history books for young people, minimized, or explained away as retaliation for Japan's own losses. An example is the so-called Rape of Nanking, which occurred during Japan's occupation of China in 1937 and which drew international condemnation. Japanese soldiers plundered the city, burned down the houses, killed some 200,000 people, and assaulted many women. Yet all one new textbook reportedly said of the incident was: "In the midst of the confusion of the occupation of Nanking, Japanese soldiers killed many Chinese soldiers and civilians."[1] Needless to say, the textbook changes have touched off a storm of protest among the Chinese, Koreans, and Japan's other Asian neighbors.

There have been other attempts to cover up Japan's wartime activities. One of the most closely guarded secrets of World War II dealt with the Japanese Army's 731st Unit, which, according to recent accounts, conducted experiments in biological and bacteriological warfare. The experiments allegedly resulted in the deaths of thousands of Chinese, Russians, and Koreans who were used as guinea pigs. Japan also had a little-known atomic bomb project under way — and given the ferocity of the military regime in Japan at the time, there's little doubt that had the bomb been developed it would have been used — but there are scant, if any, references to it anywhere.

One of the most remarkable omissions is evident in the Peace Memorial Museum in Hiroshima. It is a modern, silvery, many-windowed rectangular building that sits near the city's other, more familiar, symbol: the gutted and ghostly Industrial Promotion Hall, with crumbled walls, exposed brick, a twisted

The Industrial Promotion Hall at Hiroshima

metal spiral staircase that climbs nowhere, and the iron ribs of the building's dome, which were laid bare when the first atomic bomb exploded directly overhead. Near the museum, too, are the soaring Fountains of Prayer, as well as beautifully groomed gardens in which children play; the Memorial Cenotaph, a stone monument containing the names of the known Hiroshima dead; and a metal sculpture, arms outstretched, with the Eternal Flame of Peace burning in place of the head.

Inside the museum, however, is a chamber of horrors. There are bottles of scarred and burned human organs, clumps of human hair, grotesque blackened fingernails, preserved tumors, and bits of bone, metal, and stone fused together in lumps by the bomb's fierce heat. There is a horse with no legs, melted coins and household appliances, splintered beams, charred floorboards and children's clothing, and grim photographs of vaporized victim's shadows on the streets. The museum's centerpiece is a huge model of the flattened city of Hiroshima just after the bomb went off, all wreckage and cinders, without a living thing in sight. For an American visitor, it can be a painful experience, for we realize that our country dropped that horrendous weapon and caused all of what we see in the museum. We are guilty, and ashamed.

But here is the omission. On the walls are blown-up photographs of Little Boy, the nickname given the first bomb; and of the U.S. bomber crew that dropped it. There is a statement, too, from the museum staff, telling visitors that the Americans regularly warned the Japanese of bombing raids but did not do so when it came to the superbomb. One has to ask, Did they warn us when they attacked Pearl Harbor? There is no mention of that, nor are there any photos of our fleet in ruins. But more than that, there is little mention of the war itself, nothing to lay the blame on anyone but the United States. The impression is that the bomb was dropped from an American military plane that was just cruising over peaceful Hiroshima. The bombing is treated out of context, as an event that just happened. The museum tells us that the bomb incinerated a city and killed a lot of people. No doubt about it: the bombing was horrible, inhumane, unthinkable. The survivors were terribly scarred, and so, too, will be their offspring. But the question that should be posed to the schoolchildren who visit here and who cover their eyes at the horrors is "Why did it happen?" It is not asked, and not answered. The Japanese were simply the victims, and that is the unfair message that is left for generations.

Whether such omissions and revisions of history are to help others to forget Japan's military past or are a reflection of how much Japan hates war or, as some others believe, are just a way to play down Japan's aggression and focus much of the blame for the war on others, is difficult to say. There is little doubt that because of the nuclear destruction Japan experienced, most of the people of Japan have a horror of war, and they fear the spread of nuclear weapons. Consequently, the country has a substantial peace movement and people march and protest war regularly. Many Japanese are also quite willing to admit to Japan's wartime excesses and to accept the fact that their country was an aggressor. Indeed, Japan's prime minister recently apologized to South Korea for some of the misery Japan inflicted on Korea. Another apology came from a Japanese who was not as important a figure as the prime minister, but whose words were meaningful, too. He is Sadao Koshi, a former soldier who participated in the infamous 731st Unit experiments. "One day about forty prisoners fled while under an open-air, pest-infection test," he told an anti-war gathering, "and they were all run over by our trucks and killed under order of the commander. I still dream of the brutal scene. I am making the confession to leave it as a historical fact in the hope that Japan will never start a war again."[2]

On the other hand, there are a number of militant, rightist groups in Japan. Some of them are composed of junior high school and high school students who hold "military training" exercises on beaches. Some Japanese politicians agree with America's frequent calls for Japan to expand its defense budget and get more involved in U.N. peacekeeping efforts, and they want to take it one step further, calling for a buildup of Japan's military might. Spend a few days in Japan's large cities and you'll probably see and hear a small procession, riding in minivans and flying Japan's battle flag, parading down the main streets, shouting militant slogans over loudspeakers.

There is also the matter of what Japan's critics call its plutonium policy. Plutonium is the element that is produced from uranium and is used as fuel for nuclear reactors and in atomic bombs. Japan, which has quite a few nuclear power plants, has its nuclear waste converted into plutonium overseas and shipped back home. There are dangers here. One is that a cargo of plutonium on the high seas could be hijacked by terrorists who could make it into bombs. The other danger is that too much plutonium in a country's hands poses a potential military threat. Recently, a group calling itself Japanese Citizens Concerned About Plutonium took out full-page advertisements in American newspapers, decrying Japan's "dangerous nuclear buildup." According to the group, unless the policy is changed, Japan's civil nuclear program will accumulate more nuclear bomb material than any military in the world. Said the group:

Japan already has the plutonium and plutonium production capacity to sustain its existing energy research and development efforts. But it plans to acquire even more plutonium from reprocessing plants in France and the United Kingdom. If these plans are carried out, Japan will end up with tens of tons of surplus plutonium . . . with no clear purpose.[3]

There will always be concerns about any nation that grows powerful. Certainly, America's critics fear our power and what we might do with it. And occasionally, they have been angered at what we *have* done with it, such as intervene in the Vietnam War and support military regimes in other parts of the world.

Given Japan's history, it is understandable why some nations, especially those in Asia, worry about where Japan will be in the years to come and what it might do with its ever increasing power. Japan, as we all know, rebuilt itself to become the world economic force it is today. It could, once again, become more than that. Japan's Asian neighbors fear that militarism might once more arise, that new shoguns will take over, and that Japan will again be a threat to the region. Whether that will happen no one can say. After World War II, Japan's armed forces were disbanded. Today, the country is defended by a formidable U.S. military presence, and although Japan now has a good-size military of its own, it is referred to as the Self-Defense Forces. The constitution, which was written by American occupation personnel, forbids the use of military force to settle international disputes.

Japan, the only country on earth to suffer atomic bombing, may have learned a hard lesson from the war and may never again menace anyone, contenting itself instead with being an economic superpower that does not need military might as it did in the past. Then again, the country might look for more. Whichever road it takes is up to its citizens and leaders. About all outsiders can do is watch and listen. Despite the criticisms of Japan that we hear so much today, it is still one of the West's closest allies and deserves the benefit of any doubts.

15

Getting Along with the Japanese

By now, you should have most of the answers to the one hundred questions we asked at the beginning of this book. Knowing things about the Japanese that you didn't before ought to help you when you meet people from Japan.

The way you behave when you meet a Japanese is important to consider. A good way to conclude this book, then, is to offer you some tips about how to get along well with someone from Japan. We don't ask that you totally remake your personality. It has been shaped by your culture — after all, your thoughts about independence and personal achievement are part of your heritage and are not always bad. We do ask, though, that you be aware of some of the things the Japanese consider to be taboos, and that you try to put anything about you that might not respect those taboos on hold.

When discussing any issue with a Japanese person, try to refrain from making direct and judgmental observations. Listen more, and avoid lecturing. Don't come off like a know-it-all who sees everything in black-and-white terms. The Japanese have words for *yes* and *no,* of course, but they prefer "I think so," "I don't think so," or "Maybe," when it comes to matters of opinion or when they're discussing subjects that have no easy answer.

Now, obviously, this book contains many criticisms of the Japanese and makes some direct observations about them. Those are for you, to help you understand their ways. They aren't meant to encourage you to hit your Japanese friends over the head with their faults just for the sake of honesty. Learn to be vague, to suggest, without insulting. Don't speak bluntly about the things you don't like about the Japanese, even if you're asked to. Go for phrases like, "Well, I hear that some Japanese . . . ," "Is it true that the Japanese . . . ?," "You know, Americans have their faults, too, and I just wonder if . . ."

Someone once said that when a young Japanese man wants to tell a young woman he loves her, he gazes at the moon and says, "Isn't it beautiful?" To say "I love you" is too blunt, and the young man would be embarrassed to say it, so he uses a third party, the moon, to convey the information. It's sometimes difficult for us to pick up on subtle communication like that, and it's not expected that we will use similar words and suggestions when we talk with the Japanese. It is important, however, that we respect the way they do it and not ridicule a Japanese when he or she seems to be talking in riddles or stays in gray areas.

Try to refrain from displaying anger, impatience, or other negative emotions, and don't go around slapping your Japanese friends on the back or trying all kinds of huggy-feely-touchy methods of nonverbal communication. Of course the Japanese have emotions; of course they laugh and cry and hug each other and get angry. But they're uncomfortable when emotions get out of control, especially in public. It isn't that you should never be yourself — most Japanese do accept our often outgoing natures as part of our makeup — just don't overdo and behave with your Japanese friends as you might with your other Western friends.

Consider the Japanese proverb that says, "Shut your mouth and open your eyes." The Japanese love talk, but they love silence just as much. They're not always uneasy when they're quiet; more often than not, they just haven't any more to say, and their silent moments should be accepted as another part of their language. Don't feel you have to keep up a stream of conversation. If you stop talking every so often and just sit quietly for a moment or two, your friend will welcome a breather, especially if he or she doesn't speak much English.

Remember that the Japanese appreciate courtesy, politeness, and good manners. Don't be afraid to apologize, even for some insignificant thing you may have done. And when you thank a Japanese for a favor, you can never overdo, even if the favor is a really ordinary one. It's always a good idea to follow up your verbal thanks with a note later on. Above all, learn to respect a person's age and position. If you're with an elderly Japanese, try not to show disrespect by coming off like you know more than he or she does. If you meet a Japanese teenager who's in a higher grade than you, don't confuse his or her halting English with lack of intelligence; treat him or her as you would any student who's been studying longer than you.

Despite what some people might tell you, there should be no taboo subjects when you're talking to your young Japanese friends. They'll ask you all sorts of things about sex, religion, politics, and our ethnic and racial problems, so you should ask a Japanese whatever it is you want to know about him or his country. It's *how* you ask that's important, not what.

At one time, foreigners weren't supposed to ask the Japanese about the war, or the *burakumin,* or the textbook controversy. Many older Japanese still regard discussions of those issues with foreigners off-limits, and conversation often falls into the small-talk category. Among teenagers, however, there is more freedom.

Not raising controversial issues is a dodge, a denial, and anyone who uses culture as an excuse for not discussing such issues with a foreigner is only fueling the smokescreen. If someone doesn't want to talk about something or other, they won't. That doesn't mean you shouldn't try. You'll find, though, that Japanese teens are very willing to open up to you if, again, you approach the discussion as someone who is curious rather than argumentative. On the other hand, your new friends may be reluctant to discuss touchy issues until they get to know you better — and the way they do that is to ask you a lot of personal questions about yourself. There's also the possibility they may not know much about the topic you've raised — you may know more about World War II than they do, for instance, given the manner in which their textbooks have been rewritten.

If you give a gift to a Japanese friend, don't make it an expensive or lavish one. Most people don't like to be indebted to others. Keep your gift simple, a token. If you go overboard, it'll embarrass your friend, and he or she will feel they have to match it, even if they can't afford it.

Take a lesson from General Ulysses S. Grant. When he visited Japan, he went to the Sacred Bridge of Nikko, an exquisite structure painted in red lacquer and decorated with brass fittings. Only the shoguns were allowed to step on the bridge, but the emperor paid Grant an extraordinary compliment by ordering that it be opened to him. Grant declined politely and took the regular footpath around the bridge.

Learn to appreciate the sensitivities of the Japanese, and know your place when you are tempted to intrude into their space. The Japanese did that themselves after World War II, when General MacArthur arrived to head the occupation. The Japanese soldiers who lined his route all turned their backs on him — not, as some Americans thought, out of rudeness, but because they could protect him better in that position and because to them, it would have been insulting to look at the general's face, just as it would have been with their emperor.

Avoid coarse or obscene jokes, sarcasm, and vulgar language. Japanese humor, like the language, is subtle. You're better off with a proverb, a myth, a riddle, or a fairy tale. Here are some samples of Japanese humor to give you an idea of what's acceptable:

A priest, suspicious that a *sake* dealer (*sake* is Japanese rice wine) was putting water into the drink, warned him against continuing the dishonest practice. The dealer promised, but a bit later, the priest tried some of the wine and still found it watery. When he asked why, the dealer replied, "I did just as you asked, and stopped mixing water with the *sake*. Instead, I just mixed *sake* with the water."

An employer wanted to reward a hard-working employee, so he asked him what he liked best. The employee hesitated. Asked again, he still hesitated. When the employer persisted, the worker replied, "I like *sake* second best." (It's been suggested that the worker's answer reflects the Japanese reluctance to be direct.)

Then there's the one about the fastest man in the neighborhood. He was chasing a thief one day when a friend, who was also chasing the thief, came from the opposite direction. "Where is he?" asked the friend. "I must have missed him." The fastest man replied, "He's running in back of me."

Don't complain all the time. The Japanese respect patience and facing reality. Also, they'll think that you aren't able to handle things too well if you're always moaning and groaning. If you can't handle stuff, and they hear the same complaints over and over again, you'll lose points.

Avoid arguments and confrontation. Don't interrupt or begin disagreeing without having heard all the facts. Your Japanese friends will think you're immature and childish.

Learn some Japanese words, phrases, and proverbs. Even a few words will delight your new friends, and show that you have taken an interest in their culture and country.

Try to put yourself in your Japanese friends' skin. Think about what you've learned about their culture and act accordingly.

But invite your Japanese friends to share in American culture as well. Be aware that not all Japanese who come to live in the U.S. for a while want to live exactly as they did at home. Invite your Japanese friends to hamburger and hot-dog cookouts, to chicken barbecues, Fourth of July parades, band concerts, yard sales, flea markets, and even trips to the supermarket and Laundromat.

Last, be yourself, but only the best part. Surveys have demonstrated that the Japanese admire our freedom of expression, our wide variety of life-styles, the way most of our men treat women, our emphasis on family life, and our ability to be leaders. But while the Japanese may be intrigued by, and appreciative of, Americans, this doesn't mean they like everything about us. They may have heard some negative things that are true, as well some that are untrue. If some of what they've heard is accurate, admit it, but point out they shouldn't generalize. If there are negative stereotypes, you can do a lot to wipe them out simply by setting a good example.

Appendix
Spoken and Unspoken Language

One Japanese proverb serves as a nice opening for a brief discussion of the Japanese language: "Words cut more than swords." This means that when words are carefully chosen, they can be very powerful weapons and tools. It also means that language is more than a simple vehicle for thought. Language is also, as the English chemist Sir Humphry Davy, put it, "a great and efficient instrument in thinking." The Japanese language is certainly that. It not only conveys ideas and thoughts and information, as all languages do, but it often does so by its very structure and by its subtle, or hidden, messages, which are like private codes.

Basic Japanese is both spare and rich. Good examples appear in the haiku and tanka forms of Japanese poetry. Made up of a few lines, these short poems contain vivid imagery and are filled with emotion and with meanings that are often not made clear in the poem but left up to the reader to figure out. The perfect haiku is supposed to present two strong images, one that suggests a general or long-lasting condition, the other a fleeting

perception. Here are some examples, the first of which, by the
Zen monk Basho (1644–1694), is considered an example of the
perfect form:

> *This ancient pond here:*
> *A frog jumps into the pond:*
> *Sound of the water.*
>
> — *Basho*[1]

> *He is a winter flu,*
> *Disliked,*
> *But long-lived.*
>
> — *Kikaku*[2]

> *The color of the flower withered away*
> *At the moment I admired, in vain,*
> *The passing of myself through the world!*
> — *Okono-Kumassi*[3]

Of course, Japanese has subjects, objects, and verbs (always
in that order in sentences), nouns and adjectives, just as English
does. But it has no articles (such as our *a, an,* or *the*) and often
no plural forms. For example, the Japanese word *hon,* which
means book, can mean a book, the book, or several books.
Pronouns are usually omitted, and gender is for the most part
missing. There is one verb for *is, are,* and *am,* the abbreviated
word *su.* If you translate the Japanese sentence *Kore wa hon desu*
literally, it would come out, "This book is." But to a Japanese
it can mean "This is a book" or "These are books." A question
is framed by simply adding *ka* to the end of the sentence. Thus
"Is this a book?" or "Are these books?" is simply *Kore wa hon*

desu ka? When we greet someone in English, we might say, "How are you?" A Japanese asks *"Ikaga desu ka?,"* or, "How is?"

Japanese also doesn't have the letter *l* (a Japanese usually pronounces it as an *r,* although the Japanese *r* sounds like a blend of *l* and *r,* with a *d* thrown in), which is why some Japanese get confused when they use one of our words with an *l* in it. (I finally found my name in the index of an English-language book published in Japan to which I had contributed under *R,* listed as John Rangone.) Japanese also doesn't have any *th* or *v* — when a Japanese encounters them in English words, he or she is likely to pronounce the *th* like an *s,* as in "I sink so," and the *v* like a *b,* as in "Sank you bery much."

It's not our purpose to give a Japanese lesson here, only to demonstrate how much the Japanese can do with less — a talent they seem to apply to so many aspects of their lives.

Brevity isn't the only quality of the Japanese language, however. It has a number of different forms that range up and down the scale of formality in ways that English can never do. There are many ways to say *I,* depending on how polite one wants to be, whether one is a man or a woman, or an older man. There are also many forms of the language itself. Some may be used only by women or by young people. There are special forms for speaking to one's employee or a waiter or when insulting someone; there are forms for addressing an equal and a superior, and a very, very polite one for a super-superior, perhaps when talking to someone like the prime minister or the emperor. Americans who want to get along in Japanese do best when they concentrate on learning the moderately polite forms — in Japan, words are not only powerful weapons, they can also be a clue to what kind of person the speaker is.

The Japanese vocabulary also has thousands of foreign words, with borrowed English — either employed exactly as written, abbreviated, or with a Japanese twist on them — the most noticeable. Some examples: *takushi,* for taxi; *terebi,* for television; *depaato,* department store; *bifuteki,* beefsteak; *biiru,* beer; *kohii,* coffee; *garasu,* glass; *esukaretaa,* escalator; *jaketsu,* jacket; *hankachi,* handkerchief; *hoteru,* hotel; *gasu,* gas; *orai,* all right; *apaato,* apartment. It's been said somewhat facetiously that all an American has to do to be understood in Japan is fake it by using a phonetic system that combines English words and Japanese pronunciation, as in giving a present to a friend, "Mai furendo, a sumaru puresento." It doesn't always work, of course. In our example of Pidgin Japanese, while you might get away with "puresento" and "sumaru," "furendo" could be confused with the Japanese word *fureru,* which means "to touch" or "to shake," and *mai* in Japanese doesn't mean "my" but "a sheet of." If you plan on communicating in Japanese, you're better off learning a little of the genuine language.

Written Japanese is very difficult for Westerners to learn to read. There are a great many *kanji,* or pictographs, and to graduate from elementary school a student must learn some 900 of them; a high school graduate has to know 1,850; and if a person wants to read a college textbook, he or she must know 3,000.[4]

But for Westerners who want to speak Japanese, there is a system that can be spelled out in Roman letters, called *romaji.* There are five vowel sounds: *a* is pronounced like the *a* in *father, i* like the double *e* in *seen, u* as in the double *o* in *fool* (the *u* and *i* are also practically silent in some words, as you'll see below), *e* as in *bet,* and *o* as in *obey.* The words are pronounced without accenting them. Most Americans say *To-yo'-ta* when mentioning the car company, accenting the "yo," and *Yo-ko-ha'-ma* for the city, with the accent on the "ha." Those pronunciations are incorrect. You should say *To-yo-ta,* accenting each syllable equally; and *Yo-ko-ha-ma.*

Here are a few phrases to help you get started.

Good morning. *Ohayo gozaimasu* (Oh–high–yoh goh–zigh–mahs).

Good afternoon. *Konnichi wa* (Koh–nee–chee wah).

Good evening. *Konban wa* (Kohm–bahn wah).

Good night. *Oyasumi-nasai* (Oh–yah–soo–mee–nah–sigh).

Goodbye. *Sayonara* (Sah–yoh–nah–rah).

Fare thee well (very polite good-bye). *Goki-genyo* (Goh–kee–ghen–yoh).

How do you do? I'm pleased to meet you. *Hajimemashite* (Hah–jee–meh–mahsh–teh).

Are you well? *Ogenki desu ka?* (Oh–ghen–kee des kah?)

Yes, I am well. And you? *Hai, genki desu. Anata wa?* (High, ghen-kee des. Ah–nah–ta wa?)

I am John. My name is John. *John desu* (John des). (Note: Never put *san,* which means Mr., Mrs., or Miss, after your name when introducing or referring to yourself. That's left for the person addressing you; you add *san* to a name only when you're addressing someone else.)

Are you Yuki? *Yuki-san desu ka?* (Yoo–kee–sahn des kah?)

I'm sorry. *Sumimasen* (Soo–mee–mah–sen).

Excuse me. *Gomen nasai* (Goh–men nah–sigh).

Thank you. *Arigato* (friendly) (Ah–ree–gah–toh). *Arigato gozaimasu* (polite) (Ah–ree–gah–toh goh–zigh–mahs).

Thank you very much. *Do mo arigato gozaimasu* (Doh moh ah–ree–gah–toh goh–zigh–mahs).

You're welcome. *Do itashimashite* (Doh ee–ta–shee–mahsh–teh).

Is that so? *So desu ka?* (Soh des kah?)

Just a moment, please. *Tyotto matte, kudasai* (Choh-toh mah-teh, koo-da-sigh).

I. *Watakushi* (polite) (Wah-tah-koo-shee). *Watashi* (general) (Wah-tah-shee).

You. *Anata* (Ah-nah-tah).

He, she. *Anokata* (he, she) (Ah-noh-kah-tah). *Kare* (he) (Kah-reh). *Kanojo* (she) (Kah-noh-joh).

We. *Watakushi-tachi (Wah-tah-koo-shee-tah-chee)*.

You (plural). *Anata-tachi* (Ah-nah-tah-tah-chee).

They. *Anokata-tachi* (Ah-noh-kah-tah-tah-chee).

Your (possessive). *Anata no* (Ah-nah-tah-noh).

My, mine. *Watakushi no* (Wah-tah-koo-shee noh).

What is your name? *Anata no onamae wa?* (Ah-nah-tah noh oh-nah-migh wah?)

I understand. *Wakarimasu* (Wah-kah-ree-mahs).

No, I don't understand. *Ie, wakarimasen* (Ee-eh, wah-kah-ree-mah-sen).

Do you understand English? *Eigo wa wakarimasu ka?* (Ay-goh wah wah-kah-ree-mahs kah?)

Let's speak English. *Eigo de hanashimasho* (Ay-go day hah-nah-shee-mah-shoh).

Like us, the Japanese communicate in many nonverbal ways, too, often saying a lot while saying nothing. Some of their signals are similar to ours. They nod for "yes," shake their heads for "no," and wave their hands. (Although, when a Japanese teenager waves his or her hand away from you, that means "Come here," not "Go away.") But they don't point because it's unsubtle and is considered rude; Japanese usually move a hand gently in a wavy motion to call attention to somebody or something. Japanese bow; we shake hands (although a Japanese will often extend a hand to a Westerner as an acknowledgment of our customary greeting). One method of nonverbal communication that they do not share with us is hugging and kissing in public. Even holding hands is considered bad form. Other no-no's are backslapping and raucous horsing around; Japanese men might do it in private, but very rarely in public. Japanese also rarely look you straight in the eyes when they're talking to you; that's too direct for them, and because they themselves appreciate "inner space," they won't infringe on yours by staring at you.

The Japanese also have ways of communicating with unseen powers, without using words, something like we do when we rub a rabbit's foot for luck or wear a lucky hat. For instance, when Japanese teenagers want to find something they've lost, all they have to do is raise a hand close to an ear, make a beckoning gesture, and think, "Come back to me, please." Can't remember a test answer? Japanese teens solve that by putting their right forefinger on their forehead while drawing the shape of a tornado on their desk with the left forefinger. The answer will come. When they want someone to like them, there's an easier way than pestering that person: Just put a picture of the person on your desk, make a circle out of your left thumb and forefinger, stare through the circle at the picture, and think, "I'm going to talk to So-and-So."[5]

But the nonverbal gesture most often used in Japan is the smile. Sometimes it appears the Japanese smile too much. The Japanese smile, however, is a bit more mysterious than it is among Americans, and if there is really anything inscrutable about the Japanese (and other Asians), it is certainly their smile. Much has been written about the Japanese *sumairu,* or smile, and there are all sorts of explanations about what it means when it shows up on a Japanese face.

We smile because we are amused, want to show affection, or want to be polite. Occasionally, we smile sardonically, that is, mockingly or disdainfully. But a Japanese person may smile when he or she is pleased, sad, or not amused, when uncomfortable, embarrassed, or even angry. Some Japanese baseball players smile when they make an error or strike out; a Japanese commuter may smile when he misses a train or trips in the street. A Japanese teenager may smile frequently during a conversation with a foreign teen — even when the conversation isn't the slightest bit funny.

People who don't know the Japanese say that they smile a lot because they are insincere. That's just not true. You have to remember that the Japanese (and indeed, most Asians) are taught early on to control their feelings, and not to show strong emotion in their faces. If a Japanese teenager is angry at an older person and shows it by grimacing or frowning, for instance, that would be a visible show of disrespect. So Japanese are taught to keep an expressionless face. It's okay for a small child to demonstrate his or her emotions, but for an adult to do so is considered bad form.

So why do they smile, and often at things we wouldn't dream of smiling at?

One explanation is that while the Japanese are taught to repress their feelings, they realize that doing so all the time may be unhealthy. The smile, therefore, might serve as a kind of mask for inappropriate feelings, a sort of safety valve.[6] Another explanation is that the Japanese smile when verbal communication with foreigners breaks down, something that happens frequently. Yet another possible answer is this one from a Japanese observer of such behavior. "One reason may be," he wrote,

> *that what is or is not to be smiled at differs in different cultures. Something that permits a smile in one society does not in another. We Japanese cannot figure out the smiles of foreigners, while foreigners find the Japanese smile eerie. We often hear of misunderstandings arising from a smile. One Japanese answer might be that he wasn't smiling at all. . . . [Sometimes] it is something akin to a smile. We appear to smile. . . .*
>
> *When the doors of a train slam on a Japanese, he had been expressionless, and had he made the train he would have maintained that. After all, he would have had no need to smile at those around him. But when the doors closed, he was suddenly unable to decide what expression to assume. Taken aback for a moment, he allowed the stress on his face to relax, and in that instant of relaxation his expressionlessness dissolved, and he appeared to be smiling. Westerners get lots of practice keeping faces expressive, and can do it instantly.[7]*

What about laughter, a smile's extension, in Japan? Sometimes, when a Japanese is nervous in the company of a foreigner, he or she will laugh, just as they might smile to cover up nervousness. We do that, too. The Japanese also laugh when something is funny. But while men might do so easily, women generally cover their mouths when they laugh. One thing you won't usually hear in public in Japan is very loud, rowdy laughter; that's usually reserved for clubs and parties.

Our discussions of proverbs, language, smiles, and all the other methods of communicating might seem trivial, but you may be certain that it is not. Learning how others communicate

is important to understanding their culture, behavior, and interests. If you know even a smattering of Japanese, if you can
come up with a Japanese proverb at the right time, or if you
know when to bow and when to wave a hand, you'll not only
impress your Japanese friends, but they'll appreciate you for
trying to understand their ways. Talking only about international trade, electronic equipment, and the differences between
Japanese and Americans is not the best way to get the people of
two cultures to understand one another.

Notes

Introduction: Zipangu, Jih-pen, Dai Nippon

1. Edwin O. Reischauer, *Japan: The Story of a Nation* (New York: Knopf, 1981) p. 244.
2. *John L. Stoddard's Lectures,* vol. III (New York: Belford, Middlebrook & Co., 1897) p. 40.

1. Mountains and People

1. James Sterngold, "While Land Prices in Japan Soar, Officials Fight Back with Words," *New York Times* (March 25, 1990) p. 1.
2. *John L. Stoddard's Lectures,* p. 211.
3. Ronald Latham, *Marco Polo: The Travels* (New York: Penguin, 1958) p. 243.

2. Gods and Goddesses; Emperors and Shoguns

1. Will Durant, *Our Oriental Heritage,* vol. 1 of *The Story of Civilization* (New York: Simon and Schuster, 1954) p. 831.
2. E. S. Ellis and C. F. Horne, *The Story of the Greatest Nations,* vol. VIII (New York: Francis R. Niglutsch, 1901) p. 1426.

3. Foreign Devils, Black Ships, and an American Shogun

1. Ellis and Horne, *The Story of the Greatest Nations,* p. 1432.
2. Ibid., p. 1437.
3. *Religion in Japan,* About Japan series, Foreign Press Center of Japan (March 1980) p. 30.
4. "Hirohito: The First Gentleman," *Time* (October 4, 1971) p. 35.
5. "Once a God and a Bitter Wartime Foe, Emperor Is Now America's Guest," *People* (October 6, 1975) p. 45.

4. Beliefs and Customs

1. *Proverbs* (Tokyo: *Asahi Evening News,* 1982).
2. R. H. Blyth, *Oriental Humor* (Tokyo: Hokuseido Press, 1959).
3. Robert Whiting, *The Chrysanthemum and the Bat* (Tokyo: Permanent Press, 1977) p. 150.

5. Japanese Home Life

1. *Kodansha Encyclopedia of Japan* (Tokyo: Kodansha Ltd., 1983) p. 353.

6. Sex and Sex Roles in Japan

1. *John L. Stoddard's Lectures,* pp. 199–200.
2. *Kodansha Encyclopedia of Japan,* p. 258.
3. Mariko Bando, *The Women of Japan,* About Japan series, Foreign Press Center of Japan (July 1977) p. 29.
4. "Women's Participation in Society and Lifelong Education," case study in *Reports by Leaders of Women's Organizations,* the National Women's Education Center (1981) p. 19.
5. *Japanese Women: Yesterday and Today,* About Japan series, Foreign Press Center of Japan (1991) pp. 7–14.
6. "Japanese Divorce: Simple Process in Court but Socially Unaccepted," *Daily Yomiuri* (Tokyo) (August 4, 1984) p. 3.
7. Peter Costa, "A Conversation with E. O. Reischauer," *Harvard Gazette* (January 12, 1990) p. 5.

7. The Youth of Japan

1. *Kodansha Encyclopedia of Japan,* p. 353.
2. Ian Buruma, "Japan's Outrageous Conformists," *Asia* (July/August 1982) p. 54.
3. Ibid.
4. John Langone, "The Rising Tide of Violence Among Japanese Youth," *Asia* (November/December 1983) p. 12.
5. "Why Little Taro Isn't Feeling So Hot," *Japan Times* (March 23–29, 1992) p. 22.
6. Mayo Mohs, "Japanese Kids Simply Test Better," *Discover* (September 1982).
7. Langone, "The Rising Tide of Violence."

8. Nancy Matsumoto, "The Children Who Refuse to Go to School," *Japan Times* (April 30, 1988) p. 7.
9. Akiko Fukami, "Expert Calls for Better Chopstick Training," *Japan Times* (June 29–July 5, 1992) p. 15.
10. Susan Scully, "We Call It the Toothpaste Theory," *Mainichi Daily News* (Tokyo) (April 2, 1982) p. 8.
11. "White Paper on Youth," Prime Minister's Office, Foreign Press Center of Japan (March 1983) p. 1.
12. Langone, "The Rising Tide of Violence Among Japanese Youth," p. 10.
13. "Guidelines for Parents," American Academy of Pediatrics (1991).
14. "Actor's Addiction Unlikely to be a Role Model for Young," *Japan Times* (April 20–26, 1992) p. 4.
15. Ibid.
16. "White Paper on Youth," Management and Coordination Agency, Foreign Press Center of Japan (February 1986) p. 5.

8. The Industrious Japanese

1. Kyodo News Service, "Despite Criticism, Workaholism Persists As a Problem in Japan," *Japan Times* (December 26, 1987) p. 4.
2. Lee Smith, "Cracks in the Japanese Work Ethic," *Fortune* (May 14, 1986) pp. 163–166.
3. Satoshi Kamata, "The Tyranny of the Line: A Toyota Worker's Story," *Asia* (November/December 1982), reprinted from *Japan in the Passing Lane,* Pantheon House, 1982.
4. "Average CEO Makes $377,950 a Year," *Japan Times* (March 2–8, 1992) p. 16.
5. Jan Woronoff, *Japan's Wasted Workers* (Tokyo: Lotus Press, 1982) pp. 5–6.
6. Ibid., pp. 44–45.
7. Bradley K. Martin, "Japan's Working Poor Hit Tough Times," *Wall Street Journal* (April 21, 1986) p. 26.

9. Even Workaholics Take Time Out

1. Sonia Katchian, "Zen Archery: The Impossibly Simple Art," *Asia* (May/June 1983) p. 37.

10. Crime, *Koban,* and the *Yakuza*

1. Clyde Haberman, "Police in Japan: Badges Have Lost Their Sparkle," *New York Times* (November 5, 1984) p. 2.
2. "Japanese Police," *Japan Times,* Weekly International Edition (May 11–17, 1992) p. 8.
3. "Yamaguchi-gumi Opposes Anti-Gang Law," *Japan Times* (April 20–26, 1992) p. 5.

11. What Americans Think of the Japanese

1. "Mutual Understanding of Different Cultures," Science Institute of Osaka Prefecture (May 1978) p. 2.
2. Daniel Burstein, "A Yen for New York," *New York* (January 16, 1989) p. 34.
3. "Japanese Money in Academe," *New York Times* (December 10, 1989) p. 6.
4. "Japan the Focus of America's Worst Fears," *Japan Times* (July 27–August 2, 1992) p. 3.
5. "A Message from the Farmers of Japan to the People of the U.S.," advertisement in the *New York Times* (March 23, 1984) p. 6.
6. "All That Is Solid Melts into Air," *America* (February 29, 1992) p. 55.
7. Ruth Benedict, *The Chrysanthemum and the Sword* (New York: New American Library, 1946) p. 13.

12. What the Japanese Think of Us and Other *Gaijin*

1. "Mutual Understanding of Different Cultures," p. 2.
2. "Japan in the Mind of America," *Time* (February 10, 1992) p. 19.
3. George Fields, "Racism Is Accepted Practice in Japan," *Wall Street Journal* (November 10, 1986) p. 23.

13. What the Japanese Think of Themselves

1. "Public Opinion Survey on Society and the State," Prime Minister's Office, Foreign Press Center of Japan (April 1991).
2. "Public Opinion Survey on the Life of the Nation," Prime Minister's Office (September 1991).

14. What the Japanese Don't Say about Themselves

1. "Japan Revises War History," *Washington Post* (July 31, 1982) p. 7.
2. UPI, "Japanese Tells of His Role in Killing POWs," *Boston Globe* (August 14, 1982) p. 16.
3. "A Growing Threat to Global Security," advertisement in the *New York Times* (June 2, 1992) p. B5.

Appendix: Spoken and Unspoken Language

1. *Funk & Wagnall's Encyclopedia* (1959) s.v. "haiku."
2. Blyth, *Oriental Humor.*
3. Quoted in Nikos Kazantzakis, *Japan-China* (New York: Simon and Schuster, 1963) p. 119.
4. Len Walsh, *Read Japanese Today* (Rutland, Vt., and Tokyo: Charles E. Tuttle, 1984) p. 10.
5. "Teen Tokyo: Youth and Popular Culture," Boston Children's Museum exhibit.
6. Thomas Walker, *A Hundred Things Japanese* (Tokyo: Japan Cultural Institute, 1975).
7. Masuhara Yoshihiko, *The Japan Echo* (vol. VIII, no. 2, 1981).

Index

abortion, viii, 70–72, 94
Adams, William, 31–32
AIDS, 67
Ainus, 19–20, 154, 158
Akebono (Chad Rowan), 156
Akihito, Emperor, 43, 116
Akutagawa
  "Rashomon," xiv
alcohol abuse, xii, 95, 96
Amaterasu, 17, 35
Amur River, 19
ancestral system (*ie*), 55
Army, Japanese
  731st Unit of, 166–167, 169–170
arts, 24, 25, 30, 112
astronomy, 23
Atisanoe, Salevaa. *See* Konishiki
atomic bombs, xii, 31, 37, 141, 149,
  154, 167–169, 171
automobiles, ix, 14, 15, 52, 109, 111,
  112, 141, 142, 143, 144
  See also Honda; Toyota
Axis (alliance with Germany and Italy),
  36

bacteriological warfare, experiments in,
  166–167, 169–170
Bando, Mariko Sugahara, 62
baseball, xv, xx, 48–49, 50, 117,
  186
Basho, 180
Benedict, Ruth, 147
birth control, x, 67, 94
birth rate, 64, 67
bonsai, xiv, 118, 120
Buddha, 23, *24,* 25, 44, 116
Buddhism, viii, 23, 30, 31, 44, 48, 58,
  59, 70, 116
bullying (*ijime*), 91, 92
burakumin (untouchable class), 153–154,
  157, 176
Buruma, Ian, 78–80

calligraphy, 130
cameras, xiv
capital punishment, viii, 131–132
Catholicism, 31, 32
cherry trees, 5
child care, 72

China, ix, xiii, xvii, 7, 19, 23, 25, 154
    civil service in, 23
    education in, 23
    language of, 20, 21
    religion of, 22
    trade with, 32–33
    war with Japan, 36
chopsticks, ix, 89
Christ, 17, 19
Christianity, 31, 32, 35, 44, 67
cities, x, 8
cloisonné, 11–12, 15
comic books (*manga*), 68–69, 76
communication, nonverbal, xi, 184–185
communism, xvi
companies, Japanese, 101, 107
computers, xiv, xx
constitution, postwar, viii, xi, 38–39, 55, 63, 171
consumer goods, viii, 15
cram schools (*juku*), *84,* 85, 86, 88, 99
creativity, 112
crime, vii, xviii, 124–126, 135
    youth, 90, 91, 96
culture, xvii, xviii, 15, 24, 33, 44, 45, 50, 107, 161
    American, 151, 173
    and behavior, xi, 49, 73, 130, 133, 147, 157, 158, 159, 173–178, 187, 188
    and change, 58
    and home life, 50
    popular, 78, 162
    and smallness, 10–12
    and work styles, 107

Davy, Sir Humphry, 179
democracy, xv, 38
discotheques, 76
discrimination, 153–154, 155, 157–158
divorce, x, 63, 72
Doi, Takako, 64
drama
    Bunraku, 116

Kabuki, xiv, 116, *117*
    No, xiv, 116
drugs, ix, 88, 90, 92, 94–95, 96, 126, 132, 133
Durant, Will, 19
Dutch, 31, 32, 34, 146

earthquakes, 5, 13
East Indies, Dutch, 36
economy, ix, 33, 37, 62, 96, 107, 125, 160, 171, 172
education, xx, 111
    Chinese system of, 23
    and culture, 44, 59, 62
    emphasis on, 56–57
    Japanese compared with American, x, xviii, 82–83
    Japanese system of, viii, 81–88, 99
    sex, 94
    of women, 44, 62, 64
electronics, 15, 111, 112
emperors, 25–26, 27–28, 29, 30, 34, 35, 38–39, 177
    as gods, viii, 18–19, 26, 29, 37, 39
    modern, 43
    See also *individual emperors*
employment, 99
    guaranteed lifetime, 100, 109
energy, 7, 12
    coal liquefaction, 12
    geothermal, 12
    solar, 12
England, ix, 3, 7, 32, 33, 36, 144, 145, 146, 171
ethnicity, xvi
Europe, xvi, 29, 30–31, 35, 146
Examination Hells, 86

families, viii, ix, 50–57
fans, 47–48, 120
farmers, x, 143–144
farms, *6,* 143–144
fencing (*kendo*), 118
festivals, 116
feudal system, 35

Fillmore, Millard, 34
fingerprinting, 156–157
fish, x, 6–7, 12
Five Nothings (*gomo*), 115
flower arranging (ikebana), xiv, 62,
    118–120, 130
food, viii, 6–7, 11, 44, 53–54, 144
football, 80, 150
foreigners (*gaijin*), viii, x, 151–152
France, 7, 147, 171
freedom, 56
Fujiwara family, 26, 28, 36
futons, *9,* 51, 88

gambling, 132, 133
games, 121
    go, 121
    mah-jongg, 121
    pachinko, 121, *122–123*
geishas, 68, 116
General Motors, 101
Genghis Khan, 28
geography, 3, 23
Germany, 7, 36
goddesses, ix, 17, 157
gods, ix, 17, 22, 39, 44, 60, 70, 117,
    157
grandparents, 54–55, 56
Grant, General Ulysses S., 176
group, importance of, 83–84, 105
guns, x, 132, 133

habu (poisonous snake), 5
hara-kiri. See suicide: ritual
Hearn, Lafcadio, 154–155
Hell's Angels, 80
hibachis, xiv
Hidetada, 32
Hideyoshi, 31
hinkaku, xvi
Hirasawa, Sadamichi, 131
Hiratsuka, Raicho, 63
Hirohito, Emperor, 18, 29, 36, 37, *38,*
    39
    death of, 43

Hiroshima, 37
    Industrial Promotion Hall, *167*
    Peace Memorial Museum, 167–168
Hojo family, 28
Hokkaido, 3, 20
Hokusai, xiv
holidays, 115–116
home life, 50–57
homosexuality, 69
Honda, 101, 145
Hong Kong, 34, 114
Honshu, 3, 17, 18
humor, Japanese, 177

Imakiire, Kyoko, 64–65
immigration, 156–157
India, xvi, xvii, 7, 31
individualism, ix, xvi, 57, 77, 87, 93,
    97, 149
Indonesia, 7, 19
industry, xiv-xv, 33, 99–100
    fishing, 99–100
Italy, 3, 7, 36
Ito, Midori, 64, *65*
Iwo Jima, 29
Iyeyasu, 32
Izanagi, *17,* 60
Izanami, *17,* 60

Japan
    alternate names of, xiii
    animal life of, 5
    attitude to foreigners, xvi
    attitude to United States, 148–158
    attitude to work, xx
    clannishness of, xvi-xvii
    climate of, x, 4–5
    compared with United States, ix, 7,
        99, 100, 101, 102, 108, 110, 124–
        126, 128, 132, 153
    contributions of, xiv, xv
    defeat of, 81, 149–150
    as fire-breathing dragon, 3
    flowers and trees of, x, 5
    homogeneity of, xvi, 74, 152, 158

Japan *(continued)*
  influence of United States on, xix-xx
  isolation of, xvi, 32–33, 159
  knowledge of, vii-xi
  latitude of, 4
  location of, xiii
  map of, *4*
  misconceptions of, vii-xi, xvii-xviii, 75, 139–140
  problems of, xviii
  size of, 4
  space in, 9–10, 51–52
  stereotypes of, 75, 98, 158
  surveys in, 160–162
  and U.S. public opinion polls, 141
  and United States, xv, xviii, xix-xx, 4, 5
  war with China, 36, 166
  war with Russia, 36
  as world leader, xiv
Japanese-Americans, 146
Japanese Citizens Concerned About Plutonium, 170
Japan Teachers Union, 82
Japan Youth Research Institute, 104
Jengo, Empress, 18
Jesuits, 31
Jimmu Tenno, 18, 25, 115
Jizo (Buddhist god), 70–*71*
juvenile delinquency, 90–91

Kamakura, 28
kami, 35
kamikaze ("divine wind"), 29
kamikaze pilots, 29, 135
kana, 21
kanji (pictographs), 20, *21,* 182
karate, 118
  See also martial arts
Kikaku, 180
kimonos, vii, xviii, 65, 113, 130, 143, 163
kodo ceremony, 118, 121
Konishiki (Salevaa Atisanoe), 155–156

Korea, 18, 19, 20, 22, 23, 25, 28, 36, 68, 114, 153, 156, 158, 166, 169
Koshi, Sadao, 169
Kublai Khan, 28–29, 37
Kuril Islands, 3
Kurosawa, Akira, xiv
Kyoto, 26, 27, 58
Kyushu, 3, 17, 18, 19, 28, 29, 30, 32

labor unions, 103, 108, 110
land
  cost of, xi, 10
  usable, 5–6
landowners, 26
landscape gardening, xiv
language, vii, 20–21, 44, 159, 179–188
  English, 76, 83, 89, 130, 155, 175
  Japanese, 104, 178, 180–184
life expectancy, 8
literature
  Chinese, 83
  Japanese, 83, 134

MacArthur, General Douglas, 37, *38, 39,* 63, 177
MacMillan, Harold, 61
Mafia, Japanese *(yakuza),* 124, 132–133
Malaysia, 19, 36
Manchuria, 36
Marco Polo, xiii, 15, 16
marriage, x, 66, 78
martial arts, 101, 118
McDonald's, ix, xviii, 76, 101
medicine, xiv, 23
Meiji Restoration, 35, 129
men
  attitude to sex, 67–68
  attitude to women, 58, 59, 61, 66, 72
  Japanese view of American, 150
  role of, x, 67
mikados (puppet emperors), 28
militarism, xi, xv, 170, 171
Minamoto clan, 27
minerals, xi, 7

minorities, viii, 152–153
missionaries, 31, 32, 35
Missouri (U.S. battleship), 39
Miyawaki, Atsuko, 50, 52, 53, 54, 55, 56, 111
Miyawaki, Hiroshi, 50, 53, 54, 55, 56, 111
Miyawaki family, 50–57, 58
modernization, 26, 34, 81, 93
Mongols, 19, 28, 30
Morita, Soichi, 93
mothers, 55, 56–57, 85
  education-obsessed (*kyoiku-mama*), x, 85
mountains, viii, 5, 7, 12
Mount Fuji, 5
Musashi, Miyamoto
  A Book of Five Rings, 101–102
music, 81, 83, 115
mythology, 18–19, 157

Nagasaki, 31, 33, 37
Nakasone, Yasuhiro, 151
Nanking, Rape of, 166
Nara, 25
National Police Agency, 95, 126–127
Native Americans, x, 19, 20, 154, 158, 165
Nikko, Sacred Bridge of, 176
Nile River, xvii
Ninigi, 17–18
nuclear power, xi, 12, 170–171

Ohbayashi, Motoko, 64
Okinawa, 3, 29
Okono-Kumassi, 180
Olympic Games (1992), 64
origami, 118, 120
Osaka, 7, 111
Ozawa, Seiji, xiv

Pacific Ocean, viii, 5, 19
paintings, 25

parents
  and children, 55–56, 63–64, 93, 94
peace movement, 169
Pearl Harbor, 36, 146, 168
peasants, 25
perfume, xiv, 76
Perry, Commodore Matthew, 33–34, 35
Philippines, 36, 68
Picasso, 69
Pinto, Mendez, 30
pirates, 25
plutonium policy, 170–171
poetry
  haiku, 11, 130, 179–180
  tanka, 179
police, x, 126–129
police boxes (*koban*), 126–*127*
Pompey, xiii
population, x, 7–8
Portuguese, 30, 31
power, symbols of imperial, 18
pregnancy, 94
prisoners, women, 130–131
prisons, 129–131
prostitution, x, 63, 68, 132, 151
Protestantism, 32
protest movements, 90
proverbs, 44, 45–47, 50, 58, 59, 103, 175, 178, 179, 187, 188
Puccini, Giacomo
  Madame Butterfly (opera), 60, 73

racism, viii, 146, 150, 152
railways, xi, 12–14
  and maglevs (magnetic levitation), 14
recreation, ix, 114–123
Reischauer, Edwin O., xv, 72–73
religion, viii, 20, 44–45, 159
  freedom of, 44
  See also Buddhism; Shinto
returnees, 88–90
Rhine River, xvii
rice, 12
romaji, 182

Rowan, Chad. *See* Akebono
Russia, 19, 33, 147
  war with Japan, 36
  See also Soviet Union

Saipan, 135
salarymen (*sararimen*), 102, 106
samurai, 26–27, 35, 48, 73, 101, 134
savings, xi, 111, 150
science, xiv, 160
screens, sliding (*shoji*), xiv, 51, 120
sculpture, 25
Sea of Japan, 5
Self-Defense Forces, 171
sex, x, 67–70, 93
  Japanese attitudes toward, 69–70, 76,
    81, 94
sexes, equality of, 55, 62
sex industry, 68–69
Shakespeare, William, xiii
shame, xi, 83, 87, 131
  vs. guilt, 70
Shibusawa, Tazuko, 89
Shichi-Go-San Festival, 116
Shikoku, 3
Shinkansen (bullet train), 13, *14*
Shinto, 22–23, 35, 44
shoguns, 28, 30, 31, 32, 34, 35, 59, 171,
    176
Shotoku, Emperor, 23
silk, 23, 142, 143
Singapore, 36
singing along (*karaoke*), 121–122
skyscrapers, 8
smiles, xi, 185–187
  See also communication, nonverbal
smoking, 54, 76, 82, 91, 129
Socialist Party, 64
Sony, 101, 163
South America, 3
South Pacific, 36
Soviet Union, xvi, 7, 20
  See also Russia
Spain, 31

Spanish Inquisition, 32
sports, 64–65, 76, 80, 86, 105, 114, 155
spring bath (*onsen*), 121, 123
stereos, xiv, 51, 111
Stone Age, 19
strikes, 63
suicide, 77, 87, 92, 96, 133–135
  mass, 135
  ritual (*hara-kiri*), 134, 135
sumo wrestling, 117, 121, 155–156, 164
superstitions, 47–48, 50
Supreme Court, Japanese, 132
Susa-no-o, 17
sushi, xiv, 79
swords, 101, 113

Taiwan, 36
The Tale of Genji, xiv
tatami mats, xiv, 9, 51, 52
taxes, 25
tea ceremony (*chanoyu*), xiv, 44, 62, 130
teachers, x, 82, 88, 91, 92
  assaults on, 91
technology, 13, 111, 160
teenagers, Japanese, vii, ix
  behavior toward, 175–176
  on themselves, 162–164
television, xiv, 51, 52, 76, 111, 112, 113,
    114, 129
  and "couch potatoes," 115
textbooks, changes in, 166, 176
theater, 114, 116
  See also drama
Tojo, General Hideki, 36, 37, 39
Tokyo, xviii, 3, 5, 8, 28, 37, 39, 70, 72,
    151
  Board of Education in, 82
  cost of land in, 7, 10, 52
  cost of living in, 111
  football game in, 80
  home life in, 51, 53
  pedestrians in, 14–15
  population of, 7
  Sanya district of, 110

transportation in, 12, 13
  Yoyogi Park in, 77
Tokyo Disneyland, 77
Tokyo Family Court, 93
Tokyo University, 63, 128, 155
Tokyo Women's Medical School, 63
torii (high gateways), *22*
Toyota, 101, 145
  pronunciation of, 182–183
trade, ix, 30–31, 32, 33, 34, 142–145,
    150
  Japanese restrictions on, viii, 142–143
traditions, 78, 93, 114–115
transportation, 12–13
  public, 14
travel, 114

unemployment, xi, 108–110
United Nations, 165, 170
United States
  attitude toward Japan, viii, 139–147
  bicentennial of, 16
  compared with Japan, vii, 7, 92, 93,
      101, 102, 108, 110, 124–126, 128,
      132, 153
  diverse culture of, 151
  drug use in, 94–95
  economy of, 143
  education in, 82, 87
  history of, 16, 17
  and Japan, xv, xviii, xix–xx, 3, 4, 5,
      33, 35, 60
  Japanese family in, 50–57
  Japanese investment in, viii, 141–142,
      144, 145, 151
  Japanese tourists in, 114
  Japanese youth in, 81, 82, 89–90, 96,
      178
  occupation of Japan, xv, 3, 37, 93,
      150, 177
  and opening of Japan, 33–34
  population of, 7
  racial conflict in, xvi, 92
  school violence in, 92

stereotypes of, 150, 178
war with Japan, 29, 36
youth in, 78
universities, 86, 90, 100

VCRs, viii, xiv, xx, 111, 114
video games, 77
Vietnam War, 90, 165, 171
violence, xviii, 92, 93, 135
  in schools, 91–93
volcanoes, 5

Westernization, xviii, 34–35, 76–77,
    93
Whiting, Robert
  The Chrysanthemum and the Bat, 49
women, vii, 48
  Japanese view of American, 150
  modern Japanese, viii, 61–73
  in politics, ix, 64, 73
  rights for, xi, 63
  in sports, 64–65
  traditional role of, 58–62, 67
  upper-class, 60
  voting rights for, 63
  working, 56, 64, 67, 85, 100
  in World War II, 72
workers, vii, viii, ix, xi, 102–111
  and *karoshi* (death by overwork),
      106
  salaries of, 108
World War II, 8, 29, 31, 69, 72, 135,
    141, 146, 147, 149, 153
  aftermath of, xv, 3, 18, 51, 54, 55, 64,
      68, 90, 94, 95, 156, 171
  Japanese defeat in, 81, 111
  Japan's role in, xi, 165, 166, 176
  United States in, 36–37, 168–169

Xavier, Saint Francis, 31

yamaneko (breed of wildcat), 5
Yamato, 18, 19, 25
Yedo Bay (Tokyo Bay), 33

Yokohama, 5
  pronunciation of, 182–183
Yomiuri Shimbun (newspaper), 104
Yoritomo, 27, 28
youth, xviii, 74–98
  assessment of, 97–98
  definition of, 76

rebellious (*tokokyohi;* wandering bats;
  school refusals), 78–79, 90
youth gangs (*zoku;* tribe), 78–79

Zen archery (*kyudo*), 117–118
Zen Buddhism, xiv, 44, 180